D1287894

Digital Transformation in the Electronics Industry

Business and Technical Evolution in Electronic Components Procurement

By Casimir Saternos and Tony Powell

Sponsored by Orbweaver LLC

Digital Transformation in the Electronics Industry
Copyright © 2022 Casimir Saternos and Tony Powell

ISBN (paperback): 979-8-88759-221-3

ISBN (eBook): 979-8-88759-222-0

ISBN (hardcover): 979-8-88759-315-9

DOWNLOAD THE FREE AUDIOBOOK

As a thank you for purchasing this book, we'd like to offer you the audiobook for free.

You can download the audiobook at this link:

orbweaver.authorchannel.co

FOREWORD

At the heart of every electronic device in the world is a collection of electronic components that range in count from a couple of dozen–in the case of a toothbrush that connects via Bluetooth to your phone–to tens of thousands in a fully autonomous delivery vehicle. The electronics content in our lives is accelerating as we work our way through the 2020s, and the component content within these devices is growing exponentially as the devices become"smarter" and more connected. Electronics are transforming life as we know it, with the power to drive the evolution of our cultures and lift millions of people out of poverty to become better connected and join the global human network.

The pace and reach of the industry –the rampant innovation– is mind-blowing. I've had a front-row seat to the wonderment for over 30 years as I built a career in the electronics component industry. My entry point was Western Microtechnology, an early Silicon Valley pioneer in semiconductor distribution started by two guys out of Fairchild, the original innovator behind the integrated circuit revolution. Over these years working for component manufacturers and distributors, I've watched OEMs move from absolute vertical integration and in-house manufacturing to selling their internal operations to fast-growing groups of contract electronics manufacturers. I then watched these CMs lead the charge to Asia as outsourcing and offshoring the supply chain took hold.

At this point, from a supply chain perspective, the industry got trapped in amber. The fact is that the structure and processes underpinning the electronics supply chain today are essentially the same as they were about 40 years ago. This industry supplies the components that create distributed networks, digital engagement, big data, artificial intelligence, and much more, yet barely uses these transformative technologies in its manufacturing, planning, logistics, and sales and marketing functions. The supply chain behind it all is analog in nature, serving a customer base and industry that is literally digitizing the world. Is it any wonder that these past couple of years have seen this supply chain break as a combination of robust growth in demand, catastrophic weather events, a global pandemic, and man-made disruptions simultaneously created unprecedented tailwinds and headwinds? I can't think of a single industry more in need of rapid digital transformation than this one.

The industry needs guidance, and that's where this book comes in. Casimir Saternos and Tony Powell of Orbweaver are software architects who live on the front line of digital transformation. They collaborate with colleagues with years of electronics manufacturing industry experience. Their code seamlessly connects business processes between links in the electronic components supply chain. Their solutions are helping the industry move from a model in which internal and external data sharing is dependent on email and phone calls to one that can instantly and securely pass data in its native format between unrelated computer systems. The resulting exponential improvement in speed and accuracy among their users is groundbreaking. Less obvious but significantly noteworthy are the substantial commercial benefits companies gain by digitizing their supply chains. That is the juice that makes digital transformation worth the squeeze. That is what this book makes obvious. The future of the industry lies within its pages.

Michael Knight

Contents

Preface

Orbweaver optimizes processes and increases productivity for employees interacting with the electronics components supply chain by streamlining quoting, sales order intake, and simplifying customer and supplier integration. Our talented, cross-functional team includes electronics manufacturing leaders, veteran software programmers, design experts, and client relations specialists with an extensive understanding of the business and technical challenges inherent to implementing software systems for the electronics industry.

We are a trusted industry resource working daily with clients to future-proof their businesses using the Orbweaver Platform. The platform provides an end-to-end quoting, sales automation, and data integration solution specifically designed for the electronic parts industry. It is built to evolve as new technologies become available. At its core, the platform is an integration engine intended to support current standard practices (importing and exporting flat files), evolving trends (API enablement and orchestration), and future innovations (technologies like AI, blockchain, and analytics).

I wrote this book based on Orbweaver's experiences working with companies involved in digital transformation initiatives in the electronics industry over the past ten years. We hope that you find it helpful for addressing the challenges you face in your own company and encourage you to contact us for more information about how we can help you succeed in your transformation efforts.

About the Authors

Casimir Saternos is a software architect with over 20 years of experience in software architecture, development, and systems administration. His articles, books, and screencasts have been published by O'Reilly Publishing, Pluralsight, the Oracle Technology Network, Redgate and others.

Tony Powell has a 20-year record designing and implementing enterprise integration and high-volume transaction processing systems for Fortune 500 companies. He has held many technical positions in software engineering and executive management. Tony began a career in global software consulting with an IBM business partner. He joined Life

Prints Solutions LLC, a biometric startup, an experience that solidified his entrepreneurial path.

Introduction

Digital transformation is the next step in enabling companies and software to meet modern market demands. For the past ten years, Orbweaver has helped customers accomplish this by bringing to bear the best technical resources and deep industry knowledge to create effective solutions. This book reflects the business challenges we have observed repeatedly along with the best processes, resources, and tools to help companies in their journey. We have equipped companies to digitally transform, and we have digitally transformed ourselves through these partnerships.

This book is intended to provide guidance and advice to promote the best decisions for you and your company. In that sense, the book stands alone and should prove an immensely valuable resource. However, we do have a bias – which we will state outright:

So we certainly welcome your business. We have history with all of the major players in this space and so have seen common patterns that work and others that cannot easily be applied. However, again, that is *not* the point of this book. We have benefited greatly from a proper understanding of technology and have a "knack" for leveraging it successfully. We want others to benefit from our experience as well. It is difficult to explain to people who did not come up through the "technical" ranks, but it is disconcerting and even painful to see unsolved problems that could be eliminated by leveraging proper technology. The satisfaction gained by mitigating technical problems and personal aggravations is a reward in and of itself. The book is part of our effort to promote effective changes that are beneficial to companies and consumers.

This book, at times, may take a conversational tone and does not mandate particular frameworks for enacting change. Frameworks have value, but there is no "one-size-fits-all" solution. Differences in projects, technology choices, risk tolerance, and other factors will drive decisions in this area. Each organization's corporate culture and staffing skills are unique and difficult to quantify to those outside. That said, we espouse an "agile" approach that adheres to the original tenants of the agile manifesto (https://agilemanifesto.org/). Ironically, this document which specifically valued "Individuals and interactions over processes and tools," has been formalized into a rigid process and methodology that is often enforced in a rather draconian fashion. We are attempting to avoid falling into the trap of thinking all organizations and situations are identical and should operate in the same manner. In any case, the topics covered in this book are relevant and applicable regardless of what specific project management approach you utilize.

Digital transformation is not just about bits and bytes. It includes people and entails adjusting their roles. It can require modifications to corporate hierarchies and organizational overhauls to address new market situations. But as "digital" is in the name, the transformation is primarily realized using software integration and technical automation. Certain chapters of this book focus more heavily on either technical or interpersonal concerns, but both elements are continuously in play as projects are implemented.

Orbweaver's focus is the electronics industry, also the focus of this book. However, we have professional experience in a wide range of other industries including telecommunications, e-commerce, consulting, manufacturing, secondary education, human services, healthcare, and others. We've not been restricted to an isolated corner of the market, and so benefit from a broad range of experiences that helps us to recognize concerns that are—for all practical purposes—invisible to those who have spent their professional careers in a single industry or company.

Intended Audience

This book is geared specifically toward management in the electronic components industry and associated staff involved in the supply chain and procurement processes. We make detail technical design choices, but strive to do so without resorting to lingo only familiar to software developers. Proper decisions depend on a clear understanding of the trade-offs involved with a given technology choice. While the impact of a given selection is not always apparent immediately, the longer-term implications will become painfully noticeable at a later point if the up-front analysis is not done. Our audience is comprised of managers who recognize the need for the clear-headed technical choices required to enact the types of change that bring the best benefit to their organizations.

Technical readers will also benefit from this book, but may view it as high level. There are no code examples or assets that can be run as independent projects. Higher-level software and solutions architects will find the subject matter squarely in their wheelhouse, performing day-to-day activities that align with the subjects covered in this book.

Organization

The book is arranged into two major parts:

The first portion (chapters 1 through 5) takes a high-level view of digital transformation and considers the motivation for related initiatives. This section addresses the environment that led to the need for digital transformation, what digital transformation itself means, why it is needed, and how it applies to customer communication and business processes.

The second part (chapters 6 through 10) addresses implementation concerns. Specifically, how to transform your business, what tools and automation will be required, and details related to managing data, mitigating risk, and considering technical trends that impact your implementation.

Depending on your background and interests, you might choose to skip certain sections. With that in mind, the following is a brief summary of each chapter.

Chapter one looks at the major challenges facing the electronic industry including COVID-19 and supply chain disruptions, generational change, and technological advancements. It introduces digital transformation, explains its relevance, and discusses in broad terms how it can be applied to meet these challenges.

Chapter two describes what digital transformation is followed by chapter three which discusses why digital transformation is needed. The "what" and "why" questions set the stage for more specific and practical aspects addressed in later chapters.

The remainder of the book describes how digital transformation is accomplished and who is involved in the process. Chapter four focuses on the customer – the user or primary beneficiary of positive outcomes pursued by digital transformation. As people do not operate in a vacuum, but as part of larger community and business structures, business processes are discussed in chapter five.

With the foundational theoretical aspects of digital transformation understood and a recognition of the uniquely human elements to consider, the remainder of the book takes a decidedly practical turn and looks more closely at the specifics of a digital transformation project. Chapter six tackles implementation as a whole, while chapter seven looks at tools and process automation. Chapter eight considers a data-centric perspective as getting the right data to the right people at the right time, vital in most projects. Chapter nine addresses the risks and mitigation strategies to consider when undertaking a project.

While each chapter is discrete and stands alone, there are overriding themes that you will detect woven throughout the book. For example, chapters seven through nine explore the concept of *affordance*. In the context of digital transformation, affordance represents what the environment (systems and processes) offer an individual actor. The effect of affordance is seen in the negative when a company organizes itself around the systems built rather than around customer experience or other business process. However, affordance can produce positive outcomes by encouraging behavior that benefits the organization, for example, by ensuring valid data is entered and invalid data is rejected. Technology does not exist in a vacuum, but rather in a social context. There is a complementarity of people and systems that is implied by the term affordance, and digital transformation takes these effects seriously in its structuring of tooling and automation. The overarching goal is to design systems intentionally self-consciously to promote beneficial outcomes and not inadvertently promote practices leading to detrimental outcomes.

Chapter ten provides a review of technical trends and technologies on the horizon. We conclude with the final chapter

–Engaging in Transformation–as a "get started guide" to digital transformation. Given the people and processes impacted by the introduction of digital technologies and automated workflows, we share some basic strategies and summarize important first steps of the journey, an organic and ongoing movement. It's vital to garner support, establish measurable outcomes, maintain transparency, and learn from the successes and failures of industry pioneers. As a whole, the book takes a wide-ranging, multi-perspective view of digital transformation, its participants, its mechanisms, and its effects.

Conventions

The text of the book does not include Orbweaver-specific products and concerns, but does contain our viewpoints within the wider narrative. Callouts appear throughout the text with comments from Orbweaver management and other experts from our organization. These appear inline in the following format:

> **Orbweaver Perspective: People**
>
> CTO Tony Powell confirmed the following: "Recent business trends have indicated…"

Callouts that are related to our products, platform, or services are displayed similarly:

> **Orbweaver Perspective: Platform**
>
> Security is a multifaceted concern that requires a great deal of expertise to implement and manage. Orbweaver's platform supports this functionality out of the box by…

Acknowledgements

A book is a labor of love involving many people. I'd like to thank Orbweaver for sponsoring this project and enabling me to share with the wider world how we can work together to improve businesses.

Books are rarely the product of a single author working in isolation. This book is no exception. T. Christopher Ciesielka and Tony Powell, the co-founders of Orbweaver Sourcing LLC, were vital to the production and contents of this publication. Their tireless work and entrepreneurial spirit resulted in the many projects that contributed to the experiences and insights shared in this book.

Chris has vast experience and deep insight into the complex set of relationships between participants in the electronic industry, their relationships, and common practices. His ability to clearly articulate this information vastly improved the content of this book (any mistakes are my own).

Tony and I have worked together over the years at numerous companies before joining forces most recently at Orbweaver. He is a brilliant technical manager who continues to amaze me with his ability to "get things done" under challenging situations resulting in successful, working projects.

The design and overall presentation were greatly enhanced by the efforts of Kerri Reeves and Justin Sheetz. Kerri worked tirelessly to edit and improve this book. The final product is far superior because of her contributions. Justin's keen eye and design aesthetics resulted in the images, charts and overall layout which is far more polished because of his abilities.

Many Orbweaver employees were involved in the projects that served as the background for this book. Their technical skills and account management is reflected in the pages that follow. Besides those already mentioned, Jake Reeves, Claire Williams, Scott Muhl, Dave Antosh, Taylor Ryan, Dan Daubert, Mike DiPietro, Tim Ferris, Jamie Eberts, Chase Billow, Jim Noone, Tim Herring, Bola Salau, Jonah Beers, Dan Markley, and Usha Cheguri provided valuable insights.

Once long ago, in another life it seems, I studied piano including the works of J.S. Bach. If anyone had a sense of how to bring order and improve the world with his work, it was Bach. His manner of work is worth imitating in a wide range of disciplines. While I did not continue to pursue a career in music, software development has given me the opportunity to be transformed by Bach's music in a new manner that is hard to describe. Beauty may not be evident in the bits and bytes of digital transformation, but it shines through in any creative activity that yields the accomplishment of goals that benefit people – even the employees and employers of modern businesses. So I close this acknowledgement section the same way Bach would sign his works: *Soli Deo Gloria.*

My gratitude for all of Orbweaver's success, and this book is no exception, goes to the incredible team we have assembled. It is often said that to be successful, you need to surround yourself with people who are different from you and more intelligent than you. We are lucky enough to have both in spades. Those diverse and informed perspectives make us all look better and allow us to succeed.

I would be remiss if I didn't thank Cas for his willingness to jump into nearly any project with me over the last few decades. This book is another of those wild ideas. Final thanks go to my family, especially my wife Jenn, who shoulders more than her fair share of the load at home to allow me to pursue these endeavors on our behalf.

1

Introduction: A Changing World

Digital transformation is about change. It's right there in the name. But it is change that is initiated in response to other changes in the business environment, in the global economy, the people involved in business, and in the technological landscape. Digital transformation done right is not about change for change's sake. It is about identifying critical areas of business that can be improved by selectively introducing technological solutions in a way that can demonstrably improve a business's outcomes.

Business leaders have the daunting task of steering their organizations through this tumultuous environment where everything is being revamped at a progressively increasing rate. They need to take definitive action to avoid being left behind as the rest of the industry upgrades on various fronts. They also need to resist the urge to enact initiatives that may result in changes that worsen their business position. The tension created by a clear need to act without an obvious general-purpose roadmap to move forward has left many leaders in a quandary. Some grasp wildly to adopt a headline-grabbing technology or platform, hoping this will generate "disruptive" success. Others recede from the action, claim "business-as-usual" should continue unchanged, and fall behind as their business models become increasingly misaligned with business objectives and customer expectations. These extremes are not ideal or necessary. There is a path forward, but it must be determined by surveying the industry as a whole, and each business, in particular, judiciously applying the best technical solutions for adjusting course. These necessary technical changes are at the heart of digital transformation, a natural outgrowth of resources and constraints imposed by the business environment.

The electronics industry is a fast-growing, rapidly-changing segment of the global economy. The top 50 North American Distributors have over $75 billion of revenue per year in recent years[1]. The global active electronics market is valued at over $270 billion and is expected to grow as much as 10% per year for the next several years.[2] While growth proceeds, cycles of innovation and increased productivity continue, as observed by economists at the Bureau of Labor Statistics:

> "...periods of innovation are initially associated with a surge in business start-ups, followed by
>
> increased experimentation that leads to rising dispersion potentially with declining aggregate productivity growth, and then a shakeout process that results in higher productivity growth and declining productivity dispersion."[3]

---

1 https://www.ecianow.org/assets/docs/Stats/Trends/ESNA-Top50-2021-Digital%20ECIA%20Report.pdf

2 https://www.grandviewresearch.com/industry-analysis/active-electronic-components-market

3 https://www.bls.gov/osmr/research-papers/2021/pdf/ec210070.pdf

The exact connection between innovation, productivity, and related dispersion is unclear. Certainly, organizations that innovate effectively are positioned to succeed and prosper once a shakeout occurs. The electronics industry is a highly competitive, well-established market that is facing changes on numerous fronts. This instability forces businesses to re-evaluate existing strategies and re-align efforts to communicate and collaborate with their customers more successfully.

This book is directed toward professionals working in this challenging space and has been designed to help them navigate the landscape to manage their businesses through times of unprecedented change successfully. It starts with understanding key areas that are bringing about significant changes in the industry.

Trends Affecting the Electronics Industry

Changes facing business leaders are not limited to one particular area. Geo-political shifts, subsidies, tariffs, and supply chain shocks have driven manufacturing patterns of off-shoring and subsequent on-shoring. Demographic changes including globalization and generational shifts have modified consumer patterns as well as employee makeup. Technological changes continue to disrupt traditional business models. These changes are widely varied. Some are the gradual acceleration of long-seen trends, while others have resulted from occurrences that could not have been reliably forecasted or predicted like the global COVID-19 pandemic beginning in March of 2020.

COVID-19 and Supply Chain Disruptions

One U.S. government study cited four effects of the pandemic on the electronics industry:

- Increasing counterfeit tracking,

- shipping delays,

- consumer behavior, and

- environmental viewpoints.[4]

Counterfeiting, while a perennial problem in the industry, took a back seat to more pressing concerns. The remaining effects listed above can be summarized under the heading "Supply Chain Disruption." Major supply chain disruptions occurred as a result of COVID-19 itself. Government shutdowns and legal actions enacted in response to the pandemic exacerbated these problems. COVID-19 radically modified the entire U.S. economy:

> "These are times of rapid transition for the U.S. economy. With the winding down of the worst of the pandemic, businesses have added jobs at a rate of 540,000 per month since January [2021]. Many consumers are making large purchases with savings accumulated during the pandemic, sending new home sales to their highest level in 14 years and auto sales to their highest level in 15 years.
>
> While a fast pivot to growth is good news for businesses and workers, it also creates challenges...Some businesses report that they have been unable to hire quickly enough to keep pace with their rising need for workers, leading to a record 8.3 million job openings in April. Others do not have enough of their products in inventory to avoid running out of stock. The situation has been especially difficult for businesses with complex supply chains, as their production is

---

4 https://www.ncbi.nlm.nih.gov/pmc/articles/
PMC8014102/#exsy12677-sec-0020

vulnerable to disruption due to shortages of inputs from other businesses."[5]

The electronics industry relies upon complex, highly optimized supply chains, and therefore was especially hard hit. Consumers are not particularly sensitive to the price and availability of electronic components themselves. Still, they are very attuned to the products they depend on such as mobile devices, household appliances, and automobiles. The White House report cited above highlights this concern specifically with semiconductors used in the automotive sector:

"A key reason for the acute problems in motor vehicles is that automakers appear to have underestimated demand for their products after the start of the pandemic. Expecting weak demand, they canceled orders of semiconductors, an item with a long lead time and with a secular increase in demand from other industries. This problem is compounded by the fragmentation in recent decades of the auto supply chain across many countries and firms. This phenomenon has made it difficult for automakers to trace the root causes of bottlenecks, since for example a semiconductor may be designed by one firm, manufactured by a second firm, embedded into a component (such as an airbag) by a third supplier, and only then delivered to an automaker's assembly plant. In most cases, neither the automaker nor the semiconductor manufacturer can trace what goes on in these intermediate layers (or "tiers") of the supply chain, due in part to lack of trust among parties in supply chains, who fear that the information might be used to replace them or to bargain for a price reduction. While these problems are

---

5 https://www.whitehouse.gov/cea/blog/2021/06/17/
why-the-pandemic-has-disrupted-supply-chains/

most acute in semiconductors, they are found in other parts of the auto supply chain as well."[6]

Orbweaver Perspective: Electronics Industry

CEO Chris Ciesielka highlights the roles and relationships between companies in the electronics industry: "The Electronics Industry (also known as the "The Electronics Manufacturing Industry" or simply "EMS") that Orbweaver participates in is comprised of over 15,000 companies involved in the production of electronic devices. Company transactions in aggregate are considered as part of the electronics supply chain. Individual electronic components find their way to end users typically through a series of transactions among industry participants who can be classified by their role in the supply chain. Component manufacturers or suppliers provide parts to franchised and independent distributors. Distributors provide parts to contract manufacturers (CMs). Contract manufacturers provide assemblies to Original Equipment Manufacturers (OEMs) that sell goods to end users."

The wide range of economic fluctuations causes immense strain on established industries, especially those built on outdated, inflexible business practices. On the best of days, the electronics industry faces challenges related to component shortages, parts counterfeiting, and general product lifecycle concerns. Severe uncertainty and market changes of the last several years have pushed segments of the industry to a breaking point. The answer to these challenges lies in reimagining business practices to be better aligned with current challenges and make them inherently more flexible, dynamic, and responsive to future demands.

---

6 https://www.whitehouse.gov/cea/blog/2021/06/17/why-the-pandemic-has-disrupted-supply-chains/

Internal Effects of Supply Chain Disruptions

News related to supply chain disruptions tends to focus on their effects on consumers. Disruptions result in shortages of consumer goods, inflation, and related calls for government intervention. Less discussed are the specific effects seen within businesses themselves. The effects are particularly evident in supply chains that have been progressively centralized in recent years and optimized to "just-in-time" efficiency. These include:

- **Extended component lead times.** Lead times reached record highs in 2021. The purchase and subsequent delivery of components occur at numerous levels between multiple parties for a single product. Any disruptions ripple to affect all participants, which compounds resultant adverse effects. Many of the factors that follow are a manifestation of the non-redundant, brittle interdependencies among industry participants.

- **Downstream halts to production.** Inventory shortages of upstream products prevented production from occurring on dependent products.

- **Inventory variability.** Shortages result when components cannot be purchased. Purchasing practices become more cautious, and excess "buffer inventories" of essential parts are subsequently amassed to address possible later disruptions. Optimization techniques tend to rely on activity maintained within a clearly identified range. These optimization practices (ironically) fail to provide their intended benefit when radical shifts in the market occur. The result is a decidedly suboptimal outcome.

- **Unpredictable supply and demand.** Adjustments to optimization practices in a changing environment are dependent on forecasting. However, forecasting and predictive techniques are based on historical patterns. Prediction becomes extremely difficult as unprecedented shortages appear in various areas and buyers alter their practices in response.

- **Effects on employees.** A significant amount of fatigue occurs due to non-industry-specific concerns relating to COVID-19 and personal finance. Additional on-the-job pressure that results from supply chain disruptions only adds to the stress. Suboptimal performance and strained personal/ business relationships pushed a wave of resignations that result in lost productivity, increased recruitment and training costs, and a general decline in company culture.

- **Lost revenue.** Needless to say, the net effect of the confusion and inefficiency introduced into the supply chain results in lost revenue throughout the organization. Other adverse financial effects include inefficient inventory practices due to uncertainty, emergency purchasing of parts at a premium, and inefficient revamping of teams and systems in an attempt to respond to the disruptions.

- **Contract violations.** Fines or contract fees can be applied for failing to meet contractual obligations. Again, this can impact revenue and become an immense distraction as resources are deployed to address these problems rather than focusing on core business goals.

This is not an exhaustive list, but these examples illustrate the interconnecting concerns that impact an organization and its performance in subtle, damaging ways when the supply chain is not operating as expected.

Generational and Geographical Changes

Millennials are now very much a part of the workforce, and Generation Z is not far behind. Younger employees and consumers bring a set of expectations based on their life experiences that differ starkly from previous generations. They are technologically savvy and, in many cases, prefer electronic transactions to traditional phone calls and interpersonal exchanges. Businesses are adjusting their practices to better align with demographic expectations and these generations' growing economic clout.

The makeup of the workforce is increasingly more diverse and globalized. In addition, industry centralization of manufacturing in the wake of supply chain disruptions has given way to the on-shoring trend to reduce the impact of foreign concerns. Onshoring also provides the ability to more closely monitor quality, improve lead time, and reduce inventory levels. While shifts will undoubtedly occur, specific geographical shifts remain unclear. Organizations need to consider their focus and prepare for additional changes in the future.

Technology to the ... Rescue?

A myriad of new technological advancements have emerged and are touted as solutions to problems the electronics industry faces. These include cloud computing, the internet of things (IoT), artificial intelligence (AI), machine learning (ML), computer vision (CV), and blockchain, among others. Savvy business leaders have recognized the reality – though new technologies indeed are revolutionary, their adoption and application in business are not a guarantee of success. Nevertheless, there are numerous examples of disruptive technologies causing seismic changes to various industries. The electronics industry is no different. It has been transformed and will continue to be transformed. This raises a vital question: how can we successfully leverage technology to meet customer needs and drive business success effectively?

Digital Transformation in the Electronics Industry

At the time of this writing, Wikipedia's definition captures the essence of digital transformation with minimal hype:

> "Digital transformation (DX) is the adoption of digital technology by a company.
>
> Common goals for its implementation are to improve efficiency, value or innovation."[7]

April Walker of Microsoft elaborates:

> "Digital transformation is not just 'doing digital.' Digital transformation is a deliberate, strategic repositioning of one's business in today's digital economy."[8]

Digital transformation is more than traditional technology adoption. In the early days of the internet, it was enough that a company simply bought personal computers, set up networking, and made browsers, word processors, and spreadsheets available. The path was straightforward, and the efficiencies gained were immediate. The low-hanging fruit is gone, but immense opportunities are still available to those with the imagination and ability to embrace and execute them. Modern digital transformation is focused on rethinking business processes and using technology to improve performance outcomes. And contrary to rhetoric about "disruptive"

---

7 https://en.wikipedia.org/wiki/Digital_transformation
8 https://hbr.org/2021/08/where-digital-transformations-go-wrong-in-small-and-midsize-companies

technologies that upend entire industries overnight, digital transformation, at its best, is often far more targeted and straightforward.

Orbweaver Perspective: People

CTO Tony Powell describes Orbweaver's pragmatic perspective on digital transformation:

"Our approach to digital transformation is to start small and address that pain point. Whatever ambitions you might have for a digital transformation, you can't jump right to the end of some total re-imagination of business processes. You start with the basics. Digitize the data you're transferring on email and spreadsheets so it is organized and integrated in a form that flows automatically throughout your supply chain."

In general, digital transformation can be thought of as a progressive application of technologies to meet business goals. The initial stages simply involve ensuring resources are in a digital format and the corresponding infrastructure is in place. Later stages leverage aspects of computers that provide better outcomes far more specific to a given business and end user. This progression starts with essential digitization, proceeds to organize digitized data and create related automation, and, finally, be reshaped to transform an aspect of the business. This can be thought through using the familiar concepts of documents and communications related to business processes.

While "transformation" suggests gradual change, the term "disruption" - indicating sudden, radical change - is frequently associated with digital transformation. A small startup can wage a revolutionary takeover of an entire industry that had been unresponsive to customer demands or unaware of the changing business environment. As examples, Amazon, Uber, and Airbnb have upended entire industries, undeniable success stories worthy of serious consideration. But opportunities for successful revolutionary change are few and far between; these require the right person at the right place and time under the right circumstances. There are many examples of businesses that systematically and incrementally implement changes that improve processes, drive productivity and increase profitability. These less risky alternatives are more plausible for execution within large organizations. Also note, that the magnitude of the challenge being faced does not dictate the magnitude of the respective response. A well-executed, precisely positioned modification to a business can result in an immense difference in outcomes.

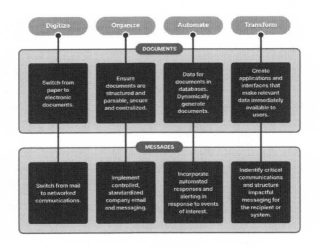

Diagram 1.1

While general, this illustration provides a framework for considering business processes in the electronics industry. For example, the creation of a bill of materials (BOM) document or the standard business process of inviting suppliers to a bidding process (request for quote or RFQ) can likewise be represented by a group of actors using a software platform in

...at is quick, easy to use, auditable, secure, and in most ways, superior to the way business was done traditionally.

At first glance, this presentation might appear to be significantly less impressive in its requirement for adoption of new technologies, but this is not the case. Uncritical adoption of the latest technologies is, of course, counterproductive. However, numerous aspects of everyday business can benefit from the latest platforms and headline-making advances. Machine learning is one significant example.

Machine Learning and Alternatives

Machine learning (ML) involves the study of computer algorithms that can improve automatically as additional data is provided. ML models have produced impressive results, but overhyped solutions coupled with muddled comparisons to science fiction have forced people into one of two camps: those who believe ML will solve everything and replace every human interaction, and those who dismiss working examples as mere parlor tricks or isolated innovations. The truth is much more nuanced.

Computers are excellent for performing pattern matching on well-defined, restricted data sets in a limited problem space. They easily outperform humans in speed, and in some cases, in accuracy. Machine learning is simply one more set of techniques capable of doing pattern matching. ML models appear to do magic in limited problem domains with sufficient training data. There are undoubtedly parts of any business that would benefit from automated pattern matching. There are a vast number of electronic parts in production today which means there is a great deal of data available. Electronic parts are also a relatively well-understood and specific domain. With those constraints in mind, it isn't difficult to imagine an application for ML to perform the classification of electronic parts. ML has a very definite contribution that it can make to automating this task in specific contexts.

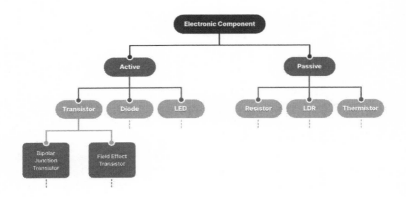

Diagram 1.2

However, consider the goal of the ML algorithm just mentioned: to classify electronic parts. In many contexts, we already have the classification information available in a specification, spreadsheet or database. In many cases, the challenge is to make relevant data available as quickly and efficiently as possible. And this is where you notice a shift in the conversation. We started with machine learning as an interesting innovative technology, and considered how it might be leveraged. Then we switched gears to consider, *what is the business goal we are trying to achieve?* Herein lies the focus of digital transformation. It is not the misinformed, uncritical adoption of technologies in the blind hope that such thrashing will result in disruptive success. It is the strategic, disciplined analysis of business practices and how they can be updated and aligned using technology to operate at peak efficiency in a new dynamic environment.

People – Agents of Change

At times, the focus of digital transformation highlights the "digital," meaning computers, software and technology in general, at the expense of "transformation." More specifically, we disregard the transformation of businesses made up of people providing value to others. Transformation requires people. Transformation affects people. Digital transformation is fundamentally directed toward business goals represented by people taking concrete actions like buying, selling, searching, retrieving, and analyzing. Those involved in digital transformation projects must not be led away from fundamental management and interpersonal engagement that need to accompany the work. The following specific roles are integral to any digital transformation initiative.

The champion recognizes the company's need to change, and is willing to expend a great deal of energy to enact real change within the company. Since most organizations resist change, the champion must be decisive, dynamic, and vocal. The champion helps the organization come to terms with the reality of the everyday challenges they face and enables them to see the benefits that will be realized through a digital transformation initiative.

Senior management is often not interested in the implementation details of digital transformation, but is extremely concerned with potential risks and positive outcomes of related projects. The champion needs to communicate project goals, statuses, and results in a manner that addresses management concerns. Likewise, peers might not be interested in project specifics, but are highly concerned about digital transformation's effects on the company as well as on themselves as individuals. Champions need to be in ongoing dialogue with these fellow employees to address concerns and ensure work done is appropriately aligned with all business objectives.

Adequate adoption and buy-in go a long way toward keeping a project's forward momentum once initial challenges are perceived.

Technical partners include internal IT staff, business partners, SaaS providers, and consultants. These people are experts in their specific realms but need to have a clear vision of the goals and work to be done. Adequate project planning and defined metrics can be beneficial for providing objective criteria for measuring progress as the transformation is underway. Technical partners generally will not understand your business in-depth, but with adequate explanation, they can tell you the best way to leverage technology to meet your requirements.

Customers – both internal and external – are end users in various business processes. They are key to digital transformation success. Understanding their perception of existing processes and areas they would like to see improved is essential. Many expensive, failed digital transformation projects resulted from a new, responsive, freshly designed web application that didn't address the business process interactions actually in use. End users provide a clear understanding of where change is actually needed.

Finally, in general, people resistant to change are concerned that computers will replace or eliminate people. It's important to realize and articulate that computers and people are good at different things. Computers can do the exact same tasks countless times with inhuman precision, but produce useless results when applied to processes requiring varying, dynamic, frequently changing behavior. Computers are best seen as agents that *augment* human efforts, not simply *replace* people altogether. In all likelihood, your primary business model doesn't need to change. Human trust and relationships cannot be eliminated when negotiating sophisticated business transactions. Digital transformation is most effective in addressing widely recognized pain points. Let technology address those areas that everyone wants to just "go away."

The Path Forward

This chapter touches on themes that will be developed further in this book. First, I observed that significant changes are affecting the overall economy and the electronics industry in particular. Some changes were unpredictable, immediate, and well-publicized such as the COVID-19 pandemic, government responses with direct economic impact, and related supply chain disruptions. Other changes were somewhat predictable, gradual, and didn't dominate media attention to the same degree. These include continued trends related to globalization and generational change and ongoing introduction of and experimentation with new technologies. People, the agents of change and the reasons for change, must be kept front and center when entering a digital transformation. It's designed to augment human abilities and processes in a way that better aligns a business to accomplish its goals and meet its customers' needs.

In subsequent chapters, we will explore these concerns to a greater degree, focusing on specific implementation concerns. And throughout, we will connect the ideas and their applications with the electronics industry which faces many challenges. Some are common to all businesses in the modern era, while others are relatively unique and restricted to electronics manufacturers and suppliers. All of them can be positively impacted by the strategic introduction of technical solutions directed at improving and augmenting the performance of people and the processes in use to provide the best products and services available in an increasingly competitive market space.

What is Digital Transformation?

Digital transformation was described in a CIO.com article as follows:

> "Digital transformation marks a rethinking of how an organization uses technology, people, and processes in pursuit of new business models and new revenue streams, driven by changes in customer expectations around products and services."[9]

Like previous definitions, it is muddled, in that businesses have been utilizing digital technology for decades and continuously have updated their processes, driven by marketing demands. Is digital transformation even a useful term? Or is it simply a marketing-driven repackaging of business as usual?

Shift from Physical Metaphors to Dynamic Processes

Actually, the definition above is quite useful, but requires some context. Technology adoption in the 1990s involved relatively straightforward actions common to all businesses. Businesses

---

9 https://www.cio.com/article/3211428/what-is-digital-transformation-a-necessary-disruption.html

continued operating as they had in the past, but electronic solutions began to take over existing business artifacts and processes. Personal computers running word processing software replaced typewriters. Electronic documents replaced paper documents like spreadsheets and traditional reports. E-mail replaced physical transmission via postal mail.

The simple fact that digital alternatives included many valuable features made technology adoption easy. Email could replace a mailing that was expensive to duplicate and send using the postal service. Such a mailing involves a nearly instantaneous transfer as well. Documents could be quickly duplicated and modified rather than laboriously retyped. These solutions essentially allowed businesses to continue to operate as they had previously, only with greater efficiency.

Incremental changes occurred over time as users and businesses identified new and better ways of utilizing technology. Web-based storefronts and Enterprise Resource Planning (ERP) systems represented more significant changes for businesses. Although customizable to a certain degree, these systems largely provided a common set of features required by a reasonable number of businesses operating at a given level. The connection between older real-world analogs for such systems is a bit more tenuous. Physical stores and electronic stores allow customers to purchase items, but the "experience" and customer expectations are quite different. There is no clear analog for an ERP in the real world. It is a digital consolidation of standard business data, documents, and auditing that allows businesses to centrally manage accounting, procurement, risk management, compliance, and supply chain operations. ERPs did not map clearly to historical business artifacts, which anticipated future development that was similarly untethered. ERPs seek to provide a general solution to businesses operating in highly diverse business environments that are notoriously unwieldy.

This leads us to the true value of digital transformation in our current context. Digital transformation efforts recognize that the technology options available today have expanded. They further reveal that automation efforts in the past--though useful--were often restricted to isolated aspects of the business. There is tremendous potential value in a more far-reaching, integrated approach that leverages technology to reorient business efforts. There are no clear, real-world analogies for such systems. They typically involve several users participating in a business process, communicating via messages and documents, and contributing to a specified goal. The technologies used to automate this process could include web-based APIs, automated workflows, database storage of various types of information, and message flow between both systems and users participating in the process. The touchpoints for these systems can span different parts of a single business or include other participating businesses. Properly designed, they are magnifiers that allow business transactions to occur efficiently in a fast, trackable manner, minimizing human error and the need for laborious manual efforts. And unlike ERPs, which are essentially monoliths imposed from outside, digital transformation solutions are woven into business processes to address pain points and optimize business functions.

With this background in mind, it is obvious why digital transformation is discussed, to a greater degree, among management and leadership rather than among technical professionals. It is not restricted to a single technology choice or an upgrade to the latest software version or platform. Transformation identifies exactly what customers need, what computers can do via automation, what humans can do with the proper tooling and resources, and how stakeholders can make changes within an organization to improve dynamic processes.

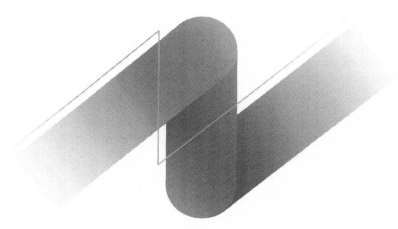

Digital Transformation in the Electronics Industry

There is a great deal of variation among companies in the electronics industry, each with different histories and cultures making them unique. However, participants in any industry are constrained by the same common set of laws, conventions, and business conditions. The electronics industry is no different, defined by a very unique set of conventions, practices, and characteristics.

Electronics Components Data Storage. Electronics parts each have hundreds of characteristics. Each part can therefore be categorized in various ways. To enable accurate comparisons, part attributes must be normalized. A given part's price varies among manufacturers and suppliers, and the price changes over time. Parts in the physical world are limited by storage at specific locations, so inventory information and availability also must be considered from a data perspective. The geographical locale also impacts date and time considerations, currency, and language used in product descriptions and documentation. All of this raw data exists in various documents and specifications, and must be ingested into centralized data storage for efficient use. In addition, adequate security and privacy measures must be in place to ensure that relevant information is available only to authorized parties.

Digital transformation leverages technologies including SQL and No-SQL databases, along with file, object, and document storage to address business requirements in this area. In some cases, cloud-based deployments may be used, while traditional "on-premises" data centers are required in others. Security practices include encrypting sensitive data, and privacy concerns require role-based authentication (RBAC) and appropriate data partitioning to restrict access.

Data Transmission. Data security and privacy are paramount when sharing data between parties. Ideally, such communications occur quickly in a single, auditable channel, rather than spread across multiple communication channels with limited possibilities for auditability, including email, messaging, phone calls, and text messages. Parties need to reliably communicate their messages with little or no chance of failure. Furthermore, guaranteed delivery between trusted peers is an important component of related platforms due to the proliferation of counterfeit parts.

Technologies that are applied to address secure data transmission concerns include recent versions of SSL, HTTPS, certificates for web applications and API calls, and relevant network infrastructure, including virtual private networks (VPNs), firewalls, and relevant monitoring. Reliable communication—especially highly available solutions that must succeed in the event of a disaster—requires distributed solutions and data replication and/or applications designed to operate with a high degree of uptime and hosting that includes multiple geographical regions.

Electronics Industry Business Processes. Standard business processes exist within the overall procurement life cycle of the electronics parts industry. For example, an RFI (Request for Information) is the process by which buyers collect information related to suppliers' capabilities to inform subsequent buying decisions. It is followed by an RFQ (Request for

Quotation), the process of inviting suppliers into a bidding process for specific products or services. Regulations (e.g., certification requirements) and business needs such as schedule, part availability, and cost provide the basis for a relatively common body of data that needs to be exchanged. These business exchanges are prime candidates for secure, reliable automation that provides data visibility and analytical insights for accurate and informed decision-making.

Conversations regarding digital transformation related to business processes quickly shift to a "build-or-buy" focus. Companies can build applications from scratch using consultants or internal staff, and operate them continuously. But this requires a skill set and tooling not often available in IT groups, the primary focus of which is on keeping the existing infrastructure stable. The availability of software as a service (SaaS) platforms specific to the electronics industry provides solid turnkey solutions in this domain.

Orbweaver Perspective: Platform

CEO T. Christopher Ciesielka describes the company's work as it relates to digital transformation in the electronics industry:

"Inside the industry there are hundreds of millions, if not billions, of components. Orbweaver moves data between participants in a secure and normalized way. We move that data peer-to-peer which means that it is secure and private, and [includes] client-specific information between two partners. We also include tools to help our clients manage that data [and] tools to automate micro-workflows within their industry, such as purchasing or quoting."[10]

[10]**Electronics Industry Documents.** Specific documents are associated with the previously mentioned business processes. For example, an RFI includes information such as a statement of need, organizational background, vendor qualifications, additional details and description, criteria used for evaluation, and schedule-related information to the request process. An RFQ contains specific information based on the results of the RFI, including details related to actual pricing and payment concerns.

Due to a legacy of paper documents and the resources required to exchange them, the digitization of documents was, essentially, the first transformative step made throughout the industry. Standards such as EDI 840 have attempted to represent these communications in a generic way. Templated XML and JSON documents transferred via web APIs are more common in modern systems. Along with the documents themselves, related requirements need to address validation, storage, document generation, document parsing, and other functionality related to the business process and lifecycle of the documents. Document creation using paper forms or templates can be improved by centralizing such activity in a web application with on-screen forms that provide data validation and consistency not possible in their paper counterparts.

These examples illustrate that a general mapping is possible between business artifacts and processes in use in the electronics industry to specific technologies. The "magic" of digital transformation involves creatively designing and implementing systems that improve these processes and associated outcomes without introducing negative disruptions and unneeded complexities.

---

10 https://www.orbweaver.com/newsroom/
orbweaver-featured-on-rcn-tvs-community-spotlight/

CHAPTER 2

Traditional Businesses vs. Startups

The electronics industry is mature and has experienced waves of consolidation. This has resulted in well-established large companies controlling large portions of the sector. Technical revolutions accomplished by scrappy startups have resulted in a disrupted industry and new platforms. These meteoric rises make great news stories, receiving a large amount of positive attention and intense scrutiny. But for every success story, thousands of startups fail. Despite the rise of "unicorns" in various sectors, many established companies continue to do business, many thriving in the present. Is it just a matter of time before all industries are upended by startups? Or are some industries impervious to new actors seeking to leverage the latest technology? The reality of the situation is well understood by people who have spent time at electronics parts companies.

In some ways, existing electronics parts companies have a clear advantage as incumbents in the industry. They are well positioned simply because they "got there first." They have a history (and historical data) of customer interactions that are not available to those outside the organization. It is extremely difficult for a startup to simply insert technology into a business built on a network of relationships in a highly regulated industry with incredible complexity.

In other ways, existing companies are at a disadvantage as compared to dedicated technical organizations. Startups possess deep technical knowledge and can pivot and change course extremely fast. They are unencumbered by administrative burdens that exist within large organizations. It is difficult for those who have not worked in both settings to appreciate the immense operational differences. Activities that take months within a large business with multiple departments can be done literally in seconds by an individual at a startup with access to, and knowledge of, cloud-based services.

Regarding steps toward digital transformation, larger organizations can learn a valuable lesson from startups: Rather than trying to guess what will work and betting the farm on a major project, start small. Initiate several experimental projects. Determine definite, measurable criteria for identifying success, collect metrics, and adjust the overall digital transformation plan while running these small projects. Each success results in the path forward becoming clearer.

Many successful digital transformation projects leverage strength through partnerships and consulting arrangements. The emergence of SaaS platforms is a testimony to this. Web-based vendors can provide relatively inexpensive, low-overhead solutions that allow large organizations to avoid the insurmountable challenges of trying to turn their company into a software shop overnight. Even if a company has the talent in-house to create applications, it often does not have the infrastructure to support the software development life cycle (SDLC). Beyond a certain point, internal development becomes an extremely costly and risky investment.

Consider a partnership between an established electronic parts company and a technical partner that has experience specific to the electronic manufacturing industry. This venture allows the technical partner to "hit the ground running", rather than necessitate a long ramp-up time for industry education. Such partnerships bridge the gap between technical and business concerns and enable a degree of independence, eliminating in-house problems caused by internal politics and turf wars that typically trip up projects.

Key Considerations in Digital Transformation

While there is no one-size-fits-all plan for digital transformation, there are several areas to consider, regardless of concerns about unique or unusual organizational characteristics:

Target Areas. Identify target areas in need of improvement. Are you hoping to improve the customer purchasing experience? Are you focusing on reducing procurement costs? The main concern when focused on this task is simply identifying candidates for change.

Operating Experience. Review the entire process to determine what is and isn't working. Make note of any work-arounds your organization uses to avoid directly resolving problems. Consider what the ideal process would look like and sketch out the characteristics of the improved operating experience. For example, a customer purchasing experience might be improved by eliminating a number of "out-of-band" communications, and be refined to approximate a standard consumer e-commerce flow. The procurement experience could be similarly streamlined. Related information can be documented and represented in a sequence diagram or similar notation.

Outcomes. Define specific, measurable outcomes. Specify the metrics to determine success and how they will be acquired and tracked throughout the project. Customer experience can be evaluated on survey data. Procurement costs can be reduced by minimizing the time elapsed from creating a requisition to receiving the goods. The metrics and outcomes should map clearly to the target areas and operational experience previously identified.

Solutions. Specific technology solutions, personnel adjustments, and collaborative business relationships are identified based on the desired operating experience. This can involve developing or purchasing software, in-house staffing and training initiatives, collaboration with business partners, and other resources needed to address business needs. The availability of cloud resources, SaaS platforms, and prepackaged solutions needs to be considered along with service engagements to develop or customize related integrations. These solutions should be selected based on their potential to introduce positive effects, such as lower capital requirements, faster customer onboarding, or reduced manual workload.

 DataHub
Digital transformation starts here.
Connect to suppliers and customers to
automate key supply chain activity.

 PIM
Finally, a PIM that works.
Effortless management of large
product catalogs and massive
product data imports.

 Advance
Automate business processes.
Create workflows to make your
data available and transparent
across multiple departments.

 Accelerate
Monetize your own data.
Instantly launch a fully integrated
online store for your customers
and suppliers.

 Analyze
Unlock hidden data insights.
Track down hidden data insights
with our powerful product data
analytics tool.

2.1 Consider Orbweaver products as part of your solution.

Competitors. In many cases, your problem is not unique to your organization. Identify and study your competitors within the electronics industry. Make sure your definition of "competitor" is properly aligned with the current business landscape. It's not a simple matter of industry classification. Software startups, retailers on Amazon, or special service providers are non-traditional competitors involved in the electronics marketplace. For example, in the procurement process, consider all participants and what they seek to achieve—especially those drawn to your competitors. Review each participant's perspective of the business process and how he/she evaluates and measures its success. Framing the question this way will help you identify competitors that might not traditionally be considered part of your industry sector.

Evaluation. This is where the value of defined metrics and outcomes comes to bear. Reports and analytics should be readily available and transparent. Remember, you cannot improve what you cannot measure. The results should be reviewed with stakeholders who might have a significantly different interpretation of results based on their day-to-day experiences. Metrics should be stored and reviewed over time; baseline metrics and historical records are required to detect trend adjustments based on changes introduced into the process.

Adjustment. No project of any significance is "once-and-done." It is necessary to iterate and adjust course in response to lessons learned and changes in the marketplace. Based on evaluation, you can identify areas to improve and incorporate changes in future iterations. To augment the results being reviewed in the evaluation stage, devise small tests that help you understand the problem better and evaluate the implemented solutions continually. Not every test will succeed, but failures are lessons, too. A small, targeted test that fails can be extremely cost-effective when new information is obtained.

While this is not a comprehensive framework for transformation, these areas highlight common concerns that will need to be considered in your own projects. They can help you design a suitable project plan and will help you schedule and structure meetings and communications that shape discussions in a way that can lead to beneficial results that are aligned with your corporate culture.

• *Target Areas for Change*

Despite the differences among companies and even industries, several common areas may be targeted for change through digital transformation:

Automation of tedious processes. It is undeniable that a subset of emails with spreadsheets could be more accurately stored, tracked, and accessed if replaced by APIs and messaging on a reliable platform. This change can enhance the effectiveness and productivity of employees by freeing them up to focus on tasks that computers cannot perform well.

Centralization and standardization of fragmented data. Essential data is frequently scattered throughout an organization in places that are difficult for users to find and access. Data quality is not always apparent, and another canonical version of that data might reside elsewhere. By storing the data in a normalized fashion in a central data store with adequate role-based authorization controls, an organization can improve its efficiency immensely, often in unforeseen areas.

Personalization. A process tailored to an end user's needs will be more satisfying and frequently yield better overall results. Removing friction in existing processes, or simply reducing the number of distinct actions participants need to take, increases the speed at which tasks can be performed and reduces manual errors.

Closed-loop processes. A supply chain tactic that can be used in certain business contexts involves replacing linear processes with closed-loop processes. A proper channel design for closed-loop supply chains can reduce the costs of recycling operations and enhance the benefits of channel participants, regulatory bodies, the environment, and the market. While this is a rather specialized type of change, it is potentially a very profitable option for properly positioned businesses.

Collaborative ecosystems. There is a tradition of a "walled-garden" approach to doing business: isolate the business and customers from competitors in an effort to become the single dominant player that eliminates other alternatives. This model works for businesses that are entrenched and have absolute monopolies in specific areas. But even in such industries, collaboration is necessary for doing business. If it is unnecessarily unpleasant, participants will inevitably seek out alternatives. A collaborative ecosystem that supports multiple market players can be a magnifier for all involved, rather than a zero-sum game. Some of the most significant "digital transformation" disruptions outside the electronics industry have occurred using this strategy.

Agility in the organization. A move away from hierarchical decision-making in certain areas can free up talented units of the organization to act and react to marketplace changes more effectively. This type of change can't be made in a vacuum and is made possible when other aspects of digital transformation are in place. For instance, if data is centralized in a platform with role-based authentication, a business user who needs access to a given piece of data can often retrieve it without a long email conversation up the chain of command to get data that's been hidden away in a manager's spreadsheet.

Other transformational strategies are found outside traditional businesses inside so-called "unicorns" like Airbnb and Uber. Tactics used by these organizations include asset sharing (which reduces costs on numerous fronts) and usage-based pricing (which can extend the number of market participants significantly). While these strategies may yield great profitability and are worth considering in certain industries, their successful implementation can only occur in extremely forward-looking organizations with unique market conditions that also have widespread buy-in of the transformation. These types of strategies can be very risky and typically involve radical redefinition of current business practices. These changes are not incremental upgrades to existing businesses, but rather fundamental modifications to their value propositions.

New technology alone will not transform a business. In many cases, technical discoveries and innovations remain essentially unnoticed until they are specifically leveraged to meet a market need. Often an organization will use outdated processes and technology because it is "good enough," losing value over time. A digital transformation initiative can identify areas that are candidates for upgrade and map them to redesigned processes and systems that people can use to obtain better outcomes.

• *Invalid Objections to Change*

If you are leading any effort to effect change, expect resistance. Many objections from experts in their fields may be worth considering. Dedicated individuals have seen the failures and successes of previous efforts. Other objections may stem from misunderstand-ings or misinformation. The following misconceptions are frequently voiced regarding the implementation of digital transformation:

Digital assets and technologies will replace all people and physical products. It's an incorrect assessment that digital solutions can replace all existing infrastructure and interaction in the physical world, or that automation will totally replace human involvement. Computers solve a very specific set of problems extremely well. They rarely address the entire problem space or do away with all personal interactions in the physical realm.

The limits of technology are often not sufficiently appreciated. Even the most advanced AI makes suboptimal decisions under certain circumstances. These would be called mistakes if they involved human involvement. They are often also glaringly obvious to a person reviewing the decision. Even when automated decision-making is highly accurate, there are considerations related to liability, legal constraints, and business implications that require human oversight and involvement in a process. At best, technology will always augment human decision-making and activity in the business realm, which will also always involve a human audience.

Transformation means disruption. As already stated, a change under consideration does not require a complete redefinition of the company's value proposition. Change can—and, in most cases, should--be incremental. Digital tools can be introduced in a way that allows the company to understand customers and processes better and improve the value they are generating. Businesses with an established customer base and market identity are well-positioned to survey occurrences in their marketplace and adjust accordingly. Targeted and relatively low-cost experiments can determine which areas have the most potential. Changes can also be isolated to a single section of the organization and monitored, giving time for other areas to adjust.

Interestingly, well-executed incremental transformation can appear relatively disruptive from the outside. But for those involved, transitions can be relatively seamless and progressive rather than jarring. Disruptive change can also be implemented effectively by leveraging partnerships. There is no need to overhaul an entire IT organization to support a modern SDLC along with the suite of servers, repositories, release processes, and support staff if a partnership can achieve it. By this approach, an organization makes incremental changes via agreements with an external organization coupled with the support necessary to support communication and data transfer. The result can be a radical re-presentation of the goods, services, and processes managed by the organization.

Digital transformation is for young companies. It's a common misconception that building a start-up culture internally or acquiring startups will enable an organization to keep up with the ever-changing world of technology. Building a start-up culture is extremely difficult. Practically speaking, hiring a large number of technical staff and eliminating hierarchical decision-making is a "career-limiting" decision in most cases. This is obvious in many organizations that look to accomplish a similar purpose through acquisitions. Success can be achieved if done correctly, but corporate politics and bureaucracy can crush the free-spirited culture in many startups, leading to an exodus of talent. A sober evaluation within many organizations leads decision-makers to recognize the benefits of partnering with an organization that can augment their existing value proposition and provide a fresh perspective.

Newer technology results in more significant gains. New technologies often inspire leaders to think about their business processes differently, sparking conversations about areas truly in need of change. But once the required modifications are identified and thought through, the result is often the decision to leverage a tried-and-true technology that is highly effective yet less headline-grabbing. The hype surrounding new technologies can obscure the actual value they provide. And because they are new, there is generally less history to draw from for forecasting the true value of implementing them.

An example of a hype cycle that drove several ill-informed technical projects was the use of so-called "big data." Many datasets identified as "big" simply are not given the processing power of modern CPUs. Vendors selling big data solutions frequently include a NoSQL database that comes with its own set of strengths and limitations. The flexible store is often designated as the organization's data lake, which can easily ingest unstructured data. Subsequent report processing is often done using a complicated MapReduce-based parallel computing paradigm. Projects using these technologies typically start well, but once data is ingested, and reporting/analytics are required, the processes slow significantly. At this point, a large amount of data is "stuck" in the selected data store, and migration to an alternative is not feasible due to the unique data structures in use by the NoSQL database. Switching to a different data store requires a significant mapping/ETL exercise. This very type of project was frequently a motivation for adopting a "big data" solution in the first place.

Many organizations have pursued this path with mixed results at best. Portions of their "data lake" remain active and in use, but significant portions degrade into a "data swamp." Data in these stores has little organization, curation, or management. The technology was designed for relatively easy adoption and the promise of flexibility going forward. It delivered, but did not adequately describe the effort required to maintain such a system effectively.

Amusingly enough, many NoSQL databases today include a SQL-like language or support a dialect of SQL itself. Many NoSQL databases that rejected transaction management to allow for extremely fast data insertion provide configuration to support a portion of traditional transaction management supported out of the box by relational databases. These innovations benefit those using the system, as it allows them to re-purpose SQL developers to work on the NoSQL systems. But they also highlight the fact that the hype cycle surrounding big data, which positioned itself as a superior alternative to SQL/relational databases, was later revised to recognize significant deficiencies in these platforms.

A Meaningful Marketing Phrase

Digital transformation is a marketing term, not a specific technology. Human language can be ambiguous. Marketing terms are even more prone to misinterpretation since they are, by design, used to generate excitement, concern, or renewed focus in a given area. Market phrases frequently provide a different perspective than the status quo. At their best, they help us to see the potential for a new way of looking at the world, improvements that can be made to operating our businesses, and opportunities to better serve our customers.

The phrase "digital transformation" introduces a welcome idea that software can be leveraged to elicit positive changes. It is introduced at a time when companies recognize legitimate deficiencies in their current businesses, encroaching competitors who are addressing the problems, and the need to reorient efforts to bring technology to bear to improve outcomes. No single definition completely captures the many ways the phrase is used. It is apparent that companies that do apply the orientation it embodies are at a significant advantage in the ever-changing economic landscape.

3

Why Digital Transformation?

The case for digital transformation will be readily apparent to many people within your organization. Some skeptics, however, will present reasonable objections as to whether the meetings, projects, and implementations are warranted. In some cases, objections are completely valid and well-founded! Again, we reject change for change's sake. However, in other cases, there is a clear lack of support or outright resistance that ultimately damages the organization. The reluctance might be due to a lack of understanding of what digital transformation is, or why it's being suggested for a particular part of a business. In order to effect needed change, stakeholders must be engaged, educated, and enlisted to participate in the transformation process. Organizational changes cannot be effected by ignoring the concerns of critics.

The previous chapter considered *what* digital transformation is – its goals, scope, and intentions. It is also regarded as a high-level overview of potential electronics industry projects. This chapter addresses "*why*" questions: Why is digital transformation necessary? Why do we need to change when business as usual has worked for so long? Why do we need to venture into new areas? Answering the "whys" and spelling out the rationale for a project is an integral part of its success. It keeps people focused on actual objectives so stakeholders do not allow the project to devolve into a set of unrelated activities that aren't clearly aligned with goals.

The Necessity of Digital Transformation

Almost 90% of managers responding to a global survey[11] anticipated that digital trends will disrupt their industries to a great or moderate extent, but only 44% viewed their organizations as adequately prepared. The electronics industry is facing a wave of geographical, demographic, and technological changes that requires a new approach to doing business. It will focus on providing better service to customers through revised processes, intelligent use of data, and the adoption of relevant technologies.

The electronic components market size is estimated to be more than $400 billion annually and growing. There is apparent consumer demand and a burgeoning market with numerous competitors. The growth attracts new entrants, and already-established industry participants are seeking to increase their market share. As the sector continues to grow in size and complexity, participants will need to increase efficiency, promote productivity, and control costs to remain competitive. Organizations that refuse to adapt to market conditions are at risk of losing sales to competitors that are focused on aligning their strategies to meet demands.

Ongoing growth within the industry is expected in the coming years due to consumer and institutional purchases of products laden with electronic components. Ongoing demand for consumer electronic is expected to be strong. This includes not only current products like mobile devices, but also sensors

---

11 https://sloanreview.mit.edu/projects/aligning-for-digital-future/

used in a wide range of IoT (Internet of Things) devices. 5G network services—as well as government initiatives to encourage the development of related network infrastructure—will also be built out, creating a new network infrastructure that will supersede that of previous generations. High demand will result in competitive opportunities for industry participants who strive to provide quality products reliably and quickly. The expectation is that companies that want to succeed will adapt to address the market demands.

Different regions of the global economy are gearing up to meet demands. The Asia-Pacific region lead the passive and interconnecting electronic components market, contributing more than $97.1 billion in revenue during 2021. Growth and investment in emerging economies will result in competition from new innovators from across the globe. This shift will also be evident *within* established companies. According to the Department of Labor (DOL), just over one million U.S. employees worked in the computer electronic equipment manufacturing industry in 2018, down from 1.2 million employees in 2008[12]. The manufacturing sector as a whole is expected to experience employment declines of 0.5 percent through 2028[13]. A contributing factor is the trend of global electronic companies moving production and assembly operations to lower-wage countries in the Pacific Rim. Automation will be required to support the communication between regions and optimize ongoing operations to address the repositioning.

Adapting to a new business environment has always involved integrating new technologies and training personnel to

12 https://firsthand.co/industries/electronics-manufacturing/industry-outlook
13 https://firsthand.co/industries/electronics-manufacturing/industry-outlook

manage processes. But the layers of technology added over time have introduced an additional, less immediate need to upgrade. Projects are required to adopt next generation technologies. Next generation technologies presuppose the use of previous generations. If a company never started using PCs, it couldn't have introduced spreadsheet software. If a company never adopted networking infrastructure, it would have been unable to sell over the internet. Likewise, if data is not stored in a centralized, managed, and accessible data store, it is unlikely that automated messaging can be used, let alone machine learning and other technologies that require readily available data as a prerequisite. Organizations that insisted on blindly resisting technological change and growth simply don't exist today. Their refusal, or inability, to accommodate their business to perform above initial barriers to technical entry, as well as the accompanying level of technical sophistication, rendered them unable to participate in the marketplace. Old communication channels might remain available, but there has been an undeniable shift as progressive technology developments were rolled out across the industry.

To be fair, a major challenge to businesses considering digital transformation projects is the need to continue with "business-as-usual" while, at the same time, revamping processes and reeducating employees to address the new business concerns. Back-office operations are difficult to prioritize in a hectic, changing business environment. However, ensuring processes are efficient and costeffective remains a central concern. Refusing to adapt is simply not viable in a competitive, dynamic environment. It is essential to investigate alternatives to doing business that are adaptable, resilient, and can scale to meet changing market demands.

The fact that automation technologies exist does not force a company in the electronics industry (or any other industry) to change. The fact that these technologies exist, *and* they are cheaper and more readily available than ever before, *and* they are being used by competitors, necessitates change. Unless the company plans to wind down operations, maintain a shell of a support staff, and provide suboptimal service to a languishing customer base, the organization must accept the fact that the technical "barrier to entry" for industry participants has risen. However, these same facts—that new technologies exist, are available, affordable, and have been leveraged effectively by other organizations—also mean that your organization can be successful in digital transformation as well. The right leadership and implementation team work to enact change in a way that accepts the nature of the organization and its day-to-day challenges as they plan and implement new projects.

Changes are coming to the electronics industry, ready or not. Shifts in demographics, economic upheavals, increased product demand –along with periodic supply chain disruptions—will strain existing business processes. Digital transformation provides a path forward by anticipating and adapting to this upheaval.

Business As Usual

Individuals vs. processes

Business processes in the electronics industry often rely on a single person's actions. This is absolutely necessary in startups or in newly established areas of business where requirements are rapidly changing and processes have not been codified. But all sustainable business operations eventually converge toward a cadence of repeatable, systematic processes. At a high level, this generally looks like a group of people who communicate, record data in documents and spreadsheets, and exchange this data to obtain some desirable business outcome. Often, a single person "owns" a set of spreadsheets that is stored locally on a personal computer and sent via email to other participants. This type of process can quietly become a point of significant risk for an organization. This may seem counterintuitive at first glance. What could be the problem with a group of employees that is effectively doing its job with minimal oversight?

There is a clear tension between relying on individuals versus enacting automated processes to handle codified communication transactions. Individuals perform extremely well – better than computers in fact – in certain types of exchanges. Highly personal, context-laden, unique, novel interactions between two people cannot be imitated by a computer. But businesses of any significant size are not built upon these types of communication exchanges. They tend to develop formalized exchanges of defined documents in predetermined sequences. Once understood, these can be digitized, eliminating many tedious, manual, human actions. But it often takes a failure in individual-based communications to make an organization recognize the inherent risk intrinsic to ill-defined manual processes that are highly dependent on a single person's actions.

Individual	Individual vs. Process Quality Comparison	Process
FLUID	Communication Content	SPECIFIED CONTENT
SPONTANEOUS	Message Initiation	SCHEDULED / RESPONSE TO TRIGGERS
AD-HOC	Message Sequence	DEFINED
NO	Scalability	YES
PARTIAL	Auditable	YES
MAYBE	Secure	YES

The problem lies in the fact that individuals are not available or scalable to the extent that growing businesses demand.

Even the best employees cannot be expected to remain indefinitely on call as the amount of work continuously increases. A person might work almost non-stop for a period of time, but this pace is not sustainable. So-called "death marches" drive good employees to leave the company or burn out. Even if the setup doesn't degrade into a crisis situation, people move to different positions over time and have life changes that can interfere with their availability. A successful business can easily grow at a rate that no single individual can match. If this reality is not recognized, the relationship with the employee can be irrevocably damaged. Last-minute adding of assistants inevitably introduces undesirable variation into existing processes as they attempt to ramp up. Proper management needs to have visibility into people and processes to anticipate change and devote resources accordingly.

It is ironic that dedicated employees who drive a company's success can find themselves in such a predicament through no fault of their own. There needs to be a recognition that the volume of work performed by isolated individuals cannot scale beyond a rather limited point. Digital solutions, on the other hand, inherently scale and can operate almost continuously. This is why digital transformation is key in enabling businesses to grow quickly.

Orbweaver Perspective: People

CTO Tony Powell commented on the risks involved with people over processes:

"Establishing an entire workflow based on one person's execution of manual processes places a huge burden on the employee's availability and scalability. Does someone at your organization hand-assemble data and email it around? Do they even print pieces of paper and take them over to someone else's desk for processing? This type of workflow cannot scale and will not enable adaptation to changing business and environmental demands... If you're taking that risk, your organization lacks robustness and is highly susceptible to uncertainty, as you may have recently learned during the pandemic. If the platform you've become accustomed to stops functioning when one key person steps away, it simply isn't 'future-ready.'"

Effort is certainly required in upfront design of automated processes to ensure that all nuances of a manual communication process are adequately captured. Frequently, the focus must shift to addressing a significant percentage of the work limited to most common or most valuable transactions, while allowing remaining special cases to be handled manually by individuals. This is another area where there needs to be education, understanding, and buy-in from participants regarding the boundaries and limitations of a system being introduced. Failing to articulate the scope of the project to those affected can lead to disappointment. But an informed, well-engaged group of individuals that understands the intention of the system design can contribute significantly to its value by using it effectively and educating others in best practices for effective outcomes.

API Overview

Digital transformation automates communication processes using technologies categorized under the heading of API (application programming interface). This rather generic term simply refers to a software intermediary that allows two applications to communicate. In this context, we are referring to APIs that adhere to well publicized standards. HTTP and REST are used in many modern applications, while legacy systems might use SOAP, EDI, or others. Well-designed, modern applications use developer-friendly, easily accessible, broadly understood standards for their communications.

APIs are, by necessity, much more standardized than traditional interpersonal communication. As such, they lend themselves to a number of beneficial qualities. It is possible to support much higher standards for security, privacy, and governance via APIs. Message exchanges can be monitored, measured, and managed to obtain superior performance and scale. Perceived flexibility for individual exchanges of information is replaced with a solution that can grow and handle larger volumes of transactions which are of superior quality.

With the accelerating pace of technological change, APIs are gaining traction and all corners of the electronics industry are engaging in important conversations. Supplier and distribution partners have introduced APIs at various points throughout their supply chain. Besides the benefits mentioned already related to codifying individuals' work into automated processes, there are clear business benefits to implementing them. APIs (and any other automated integration point) drive costs out of the sales and purchasing process, enabling profit margins to increase. They are now universally accepted as the path toward a more efficient, more resilient supply chain. There is a commonly held expectation among trading partners that APIs will be available for common business functions. Having email and phone communication available today is an obvious requirement for doing business. APIs usage is increasing over time and, in places, replacing traditional emailing of documents altogether.

The use of APIs provides many immediate advantages. Its use also future-proofs your organization, putting it in a position to adapt to future technological waves. Since APIs are a direct means of communication between various pieces of software, they provide the underlying infrastructure to link systems together. If a new piece of software is introduced, communications via APIs is a likely consequence. Organizations that have already accepted API management as a reality of their business platform are positioned to adopt "next generation technologies" as soon as they are available.

Technology Dependencies

Think about digital transformation as a series of stages in which new technologies build upon each other over time. This progression starts with manual processes between individuals, proceeds to formalize and digitize documents stored as data, connects data stores using APIs, and finally provides a sufficient infrastructure for a wide array of options to automate and analyze a business.

Stage 1: Individual, Manual Work

In the first stage, participants in a business process communicate using email and electronic documents. Each individual maintains their own documents, created in various ways using data from various sources.

Messages are sent between parties, often via insecure email. Data in individual documents is easily updated, but not easily auditable.

Work at this stage is very dynamic, but often relies upon potentially heroic effort for individuals to meet changing demands at all hours. As inconsistencies in data crop up, organizations generally gravitate toward a solution that adds considerable control to the flow and storage of data.

Stage 2: Data Centralization

The second stage involves centralizing critical data. Many of the documents formerly created from various sources can instead be generated from data in the central database. This is a vast improvement as data is centralized, validated, and standardized in a structured format.

The usefulness of databases is expanded over time as the applications used to access data mature. ERP systems, in-house web applications, and reporting systems further improve the situation. But notice that the actual transfer of data between individuals – especially those in separate organizations – occurs using the same process as shown earlier. In some cases, secure email might be in use, and there may be some automation, but the flow of data remains highly unregulated in many respects.

Stage 3: Communication via APIs

In the third stage, APIs shift the main communication transfer from person-to-person to machine-to-machine.

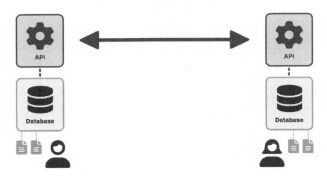

APIs can communicate large volumes of data consistently. They can be monitored and scaled to handle increased throughput. They can be designed to leverage various security mechanisms (encrypted data at rest, encrypted data transfer, etc.) to ensure data integrity is maintained throughout the process.

APIs can be extended to include not only communication with other systems within the business itself, but also third-party platforms that provide functionality beyond your organization's core competencies.

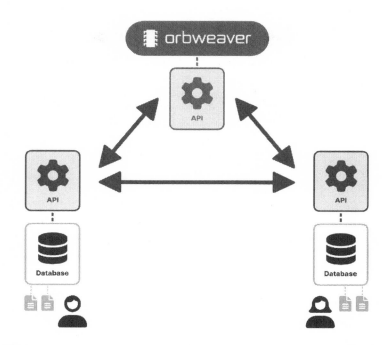

With machine-to-machine communication, an established channel for processing business transactions, new innovations that leverage APIs can be introduced.

Next Generation Technologies

The next generations of technology—blockchain and AI, in particular—are receiving much attention. While their specific impact on our business remains to be seen, one thing is certain: the digital transformation will not stop with APIs. The expectation going forward will be that a competitive company will have managed data and APIs. This will establish the baseline required to adopt emerging technologies, yielding the benefits of high-quality data applications through AI, blockchain, and analytics. We will discuss these technologies in depth later, but note that the adoption of AI and blockchain rests on infrastructure that includes centralized data and APIs.

Orbweaver Perspective: People

Orbweaver CEO T. Christopher Ciesielka sees the development of APIs as a logical step forward for the entire electronics industry.

"Embracing these solutions for a digitized supply chain is absolutely essential to the health of our entire industry. Once you're not locked up in paper- or email-based processes, the centralized data platform demonstrates a future-ready mindset. What you previously viewed as a "someday, maybe" investment becomes an approachable option now with the democratization of data, designed to be extended, integrated, and incorporated into the industry's evolving technologies.

Furthermore, by contracting your future-ready digital platform to a third party, you gain real longevity. Your organization no longer needs to scrape together resources to keep up with the ever-changing technical landscape.

Venturing into New Areas

The electronics industry has a considerable history of technical innovation and has leveraged technology for years. This collective experience is common to every company--competitors included! Each new project gives companies the opportunity to improve upon processes and services established by a previous generation. There are a number of shortcomings that are endemic to older industries, including electronics manufacturing. These shortcomings can be specifically addressed in digital transformation initiatives.

> ### Orbweaver Perspective: People
>
> A dedicated solutions provider has the scale to efficiently identify and make use of technical innovation. In many instances, as with Orbweaver, we are actually leading the conversation."

Incompatible Data Formats

A reliance on diverse, arbitrary, and incompatible data formats is a widespread problem in electronics manufacturing. Companies make the mistake of acquiring data in *any* format, often through inefficient or insecure transmissions such as mail, email or fax. Employees need to manually assess and re-enter information to make sense of incorrectly formatted data. This process is inefficient and error prone.

To alleviate this problem, companies can adopt an automation system that can receive complex data in the supply chain via APIs. That data, which comes in a variety of formats, is translated into a single, usable format through the automatic intake process. The data that is received is clear, usable, and free from the errors typically associated with manual data conversions.

Double Ordering

A report from Morgan Stanley showed that double orders recently reached an all-time high, with 46% of distribution company respondents reporting duplicate orders--almost twice as many as in the prior year. Electronic component manufacturers are particularly prone to encounter double ordering. Rising demand has made components scarce, and a lack of centralized order data has made it difficult to identify duplicates.

In many cases, proper data architecture and modeling using database constraints and well-designed extract/transform/

load systems can eliminate this problem, making it visible and actionable under challenging situations.

Lack of Data Analytics

Peter Drucker famously said: "What gets measured gets managed."

A company with no centralized data repository with real-time data updates is losing out on a significant opportunity to leverage data analytics to improve business operations. Data analytics can improve the electronic component supply chain and be applied to optimize manufacturing as well as front-end, customer-facing activities. Analytics can enhance back-office functions, including sales, procurement, RFP and PO processes, logistics, warehousing, and more. A failure to implement centralized data gathering and analytics results in a failure to take advantage of information that could translate to a significant competitive advantage for companies participating in a crowded and competitive market.

Digital transformation is intended to move a company from making intuitive decisions (and wild guesses) to making deliberate, data-driven decisions. Intuition is extremely useful in small-scale interpersonal exchanges. There is no denying the applicability in such small settings to the value of emotional intelligence. But intuition is far less useful when managing the aggregate activities of numerous individuals participating in a business process over time. Analytics provide insights for making decisions and the data to evaluate their effectiveness once implemented.

Fast Beating the Slow

Rupert Murdoch said the following about media in 1999:[14]

---

14 https://www.theguardian.com/uk/1999/jul/02/3

"The world is changing very fast. We are moving from an old model economy to a new one, and every business has to find a way of transforming itself for this new economy which is coming upon us with lightning speed. Big will not beat small anymore. It will be the fast beating the slow."

Murdoch saw the writing on the wall regarding his media empire. The former newspaper baron realigned his business focus in response to changes his industry encountered early on as consumers rapidly adopted online news sources in favor of established traditional sources. His net worth was under $5 billion when he made the statement above[15], more than $15 billion than it is today[16].

While the electronics industry is a very different industry, it's no less susceptible to changes in the broader consumer and technological environment. Businesses need to continue to find a way to transform themselves. Murdoch recognized that speed – "the fast beating the slow"—is more threatening than size. This has proven true and more evident as cloud computing technology has made it possible for a well-positioned competitor to instantly create a network and data infrastructure that would have taken years to build in the past, and at a fraction of the historical cost. There is a clear path forward for judiciously improving a company's technology profile in certain areas, setting the stage for further improvements.

The goal of this chapter is to reinforce what you already know: Change is inevitable, we live in turbulent times, and the

---

15 https://en.wikipedia.org/wiki/Rupert_Murdoch#:~:text=With%20 a%20net%20worth%20of,71st%20richest%20in%20the%20world.
16 https://en.wikipedia.org/wiki/Rupert_Murdoch#:~:text=By%20 2000%2C%20Murdoch%27s%20News%20Corporation%20owned%20 over%20800%20companies%20in%20more%20than%2050%20coun-tries%2C%20with%20a%20net%20worth%20of%20over%20%245%20 billion.

electronics industry is not exempt from this upheaval. Digital transformation is not the uncritical adoption of technology for technology's sake. It is not a call for undirected activity or "disruption" to upset the status quo. Any reasonable survey of the current economic climate and industry history demonstrates that the companies that have grown and prospered have reinvented themselves. Rather than only addressing the next wave of demands, they've recognized that change will remain constant and that the rate of change will undoubtedly continue to increase. Companies that perform suboptimally are in danger of losing to competitors that are willing to both create the goods and services that are in demand and provide them as part of a direct, rewarding, and frictionless experience.

With challenges, there are opportunities: opportunities to address requests at a scale that was previously thought to be impossible; opportunities to win customer loyalty by revamping business processes to create seamless, straightforward interactions; opportunities to allow employees to leverage their skills in areas where computers cannot compete; and opportunities for computers to operate where humans are less effective. The success of digital transformation at your organization depends on your ability to continuously communicate—not only project implementation details but business opportunities and possibilities that will arise as you reorient for the future.

4

Communication

The word "communication" – from the Latin *communicare* – means "to share, impart, or make common." Misunderstandings stem from one party communicating in a manner not recognized or acknowledged by the other party, or conversely, one party unintentionally communicating something that offends another party. In business organizations, there is constant communication internally and externally among employees, vendors, partners, and customers. Companies have long recognized the importance of maintaining a specific focus on what they communicate, hence the relevance of marketing departments and support staff. Consistent, strong communication improves the likelihood of successful outcomes in any domain. Digital transformation projects, in particular, require good communication. When implemented successfully, they vastly improve the quality and flow of information through an organization.

Teamwork

Communication enables teams to work efficiently. This applies to the team implementing digital transformation projects, as well as all teams affected by digital transformation throughout the organization. Both projects that aim to improve internal and cross-functional processes spanning multiple internal and external teams benefit from collaboration. Digital transformation requires teamwork and is also implemented to encourage cooperation.

There is a great deal of dialogue about "creating teamwork." This is largely a misunderstanding. It assumes that an existing organization is not a team in its current form, which typically is false. For work to be productive, it has to be organized and delegated to a fitting team according to its nature and flow.[17] Further, we cannot assume that there is only one kind of team; in effect, there are three major kinds of teams for all human work, identified by Drucker in the table below (and discussed further in other articles[18]).

Teams differ in the relative "fungibility" between team members, how independently they operate, and where they get information related to doing their job. Drucker indicates that the three types of teams are not really interchangeable and don't work well as "hybrids." That said, "knowledge worker" teams, like those involved in implementing digital transformation projects, tend to lean toward the soccer team model for large project teams or doubles tennis.

17 Peter F. Drucker. *Post–Capitalist Society* (10 East 53rd Street, New York, NY 10022: HarperCollins Publishers Inc. 1993), p. 86.
18 https://www.wsj.com/articles/SB100014240527487042043045745443129162772426

Team Type	Description	Comments
Baseball team (Fixed position)	Participants play on a team not as a team.	Example: Surgical team at a hospital. Good for repetitive tasks where rules are well-known.
Soccer team (Parallel)	Flexibility to shift roles.	Like a symphony orchestra, requires a conductor (coach). Requires coordinated practice.
Doubles tennis team (Innovative)	Players have a preferred, rather than fixed, position and adjust and cover for each other.	Like a jazz combo, highly flexible and adaptive, but requires considerable skill and experience working together.

Traditionally, work in the electronics industry has been done using the baseball team model. People (and siloed teams) learned a set of rules and their individual responsibilities, and began participating in business processes. This type of team is only effective in an environment where the rules seldom change. For this reason, there was a shift to the soccer team model, where the "other responsibilities as assigned" clause of each team member's job description took on increasing significance, and team responsibilities were changed more frequently. Calls for improved teamwork today tend to imply movement toward the doubles tennis team model that requires little direct managerial oversight and allows highly adaptive team members to dynamically assume new responsibilities and roles as new information is obtained.

Communication to, and among, team members is critical for a team to operate efficiently as shown in the following table.

Team Type	Flow of Information
Baseball Team	The situation provides information appropriate to a task (independent of others).
Soccer Team	The coach provides information.
Doubles Tennis Team	The players provide the information.

Digital transformation targets the creation of systems designed to accommodate all three team types. In each case, the goal is to improve the information (filtered and processed data) provided through a given flow. In many cases, digital transformation consolidates communication channels and codifies the flow of communication. It also might improve visibility over multiple channels supporting the same business process. The major differences between the team types involve the flow of information and amount of flexibility afforded to each team member.

- Baseball teams are standard operations teams. The goal of digital transformation projects applied to such teams is to improve the situational information available to each team member working in his/her respective role.

- The communication flow of soccer teams requires the coach to get the best information available and a means to communicate it immediately and accurately to team members.

- The doubles tennis team members are "power users" who are highly technical, highly privileged or both. Systems designed for such teams are more open and less constrained as they assume a responsible user base in a highly dynamic environment.

Communication is required to enact digital transformation. Communication is also improved by successful digital transformation. Both of these dimensions will be considered throughout this chapter.

Communication Required for Digital Transformation

Contextual communication

It is self-evident that communication involves individuals fulfilling different roles within various groups that have a reporting hierarchy. In practice, it is amazing how much communication is insensitive to the differences among these individuals. Effective communication encourages specific actions to change a process or organization in a positive manner. This is not attainable if the messaging does not consider the individual's motivations, goals, and constraints. An individual must be aware of his or her relationship to peers on the team and other teams within the organization, direct managers, superiors who are not direct managers, direct reports, and third parties and partners. Crafting communication that considers the recipient's context is far more effective than blanket communication describing what the sender is doing.

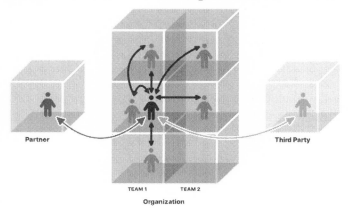

A related concern is *who* delivers a given message. In certain situations, someone close to the audience is the ideal selection. Different groups speak "different languages" and have other concerns. A person who understands the audience's interests is bound to be more effective. For example, operations staff members whose work will be impacted by the changes being made are more likely to comprehend and cooperate if the message is communicated by someone who can address their concerns and help them make needed adjustments.

News related to large scale, systemic changes isoften better received by an outsider. Organizations can become desensitized to concerns that are repeatedly voiced and have been safely deferred in the past. Consultants who make a critique of an organization are often approached by internal staff with a comment like, "Thank you, I've been saying this for years." Partnering with outside firms is typically an invaluable part of the overall communication of project goals.

Communication Affected by Digital Transformation

The key component of digital transformation is "transformation," not "digital." Digital transformation is not defined by enhancing machines or adopting technologies, but rather by augmenting human communications in the interest of providing value. Augmentation to systems and automation of processes is incidental. Personal interactions are the central concern. Communication with end-to-end users can become a marketing differentiator and a signature element of the brand experience. In a business-to-business context, successful communication can be a means to strengthen corporate relationships and promote large-scale, accurate interchange of information, limiting the mistakes and frustrations resulting from the overuse of individual ad-hoc exchanges.

Technology can be used to gather and store data, which can be analyzed and processed to create forecasts and make predictions. But until these assets impact the culture, processes, and individuals in an organization, they provide no value. Tangible actions and new ways of working yield results that are the ultimate goal of the transformation process.

Actual progress toward business goals involves concrete actions. This is why talent plays such a critical role in the success of a digital transformation project. An organization will only transform when people's behavior has changed. If employees retreat into old work patterns, much of the value introduced by technology will be lost. It is necessary to redesign existing communication in a way that makes it easy for staff members to do "the right thing" and uncomfortable for them to revert to previous processes. But no system can prevent workarounds. It is necessary to communicate with employees, explain the changes being made, present the value of the changes, and demonstrate how they can benefit from adopting new tools and processes.

Automation of business processes can appear to be a dehumanizing factor that reduces personal communication, but this is not the case. Automation serves to improve the "signal-to-noise" ratio between people. It is a mistake to force voice-based communication exchange with a busy individual who would prefer to click a button (or do nothing at all) and obtain the same beneficial outcome. Scripted exchanges by customer service representatives, despite the company's effort to provide a "personal touch," tends to irritate people rather than impress them. This is increasingly true among internet-savvy members of younger generations who prefer less personal mediums of communication.

Communication concerns, foundational to human relationships, are not particularly unique to the electronics industry. While the industry does have specialized information and industry-specific terminology, communication practices otherwise conform to those in a wide variety of organizations.

Factors that have impacted the nature of human communication in recent years did not originate within the electronics industry, though they were powered by it. Again, shifts in communication practices are related more closely to the age and demographics of participants than to industry type.

Individuals are highly attuned to the messages they send and receive directly. They also are often impacted by messages sent on behalf of their organization or those received by a broader audience. Individuals communicate with one other, individuals communicate with groups, groups communicate with individuals, and groups communicate with each other. Communication often occurs when participants are not even aware of it.

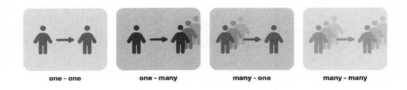

one - one   one - many   many - one   many - many

Don't Phone Home

General communication patterns are not new, but they are perceived differently than in the past. Individual, interpersonal interactions are essential and often highly influential in the original formation of a company. Remote exchanges over physical and electronic networks predate the internet, and letters, paper media, and telephone calls remain valuable in their context. Perceptions about various modes of communication and their roles have changed significantly in recent years. Consider the following quote:

> "There are three service standards to keep in mind when dealing with a client or customer.
> These include using and giving personal attention

to the customer, teamwork, and taking personal responsibility."[19]

This is a fine sentiment and valid as it applies to customer support representatives in isolation. The attitude of these representatives can make a profound difference to a customer who has no other recourse but to contact them. But the traditional customer support team—specifically phone-based call centers—is not necessarily capable of delivering the *best* customer experience. In many cases, the best customer support does not require personal interaction.

A recent survey[20] highlighted the unease millennials feel towards phone communication. Among their findings:

- 81% get apprehension anxiety before summoning the courage to make a call.

- 88% would rather have unlimited data than calls and SMS.

A phone call – *regardless of the level of service a representative provides – is an outright failure to a growing segment of the population.* Further, chatbots and automated telephone support can create frustration. These technologies can reduce costs by minimizing the number of customer service representatives required. However, an unforeseen impact can be a loss of profit due to customer churn. Likewise, user experience (UX) and user interfaces (UI) are useful areas of focus when considering communication impacted by digital solutions. But they tend to focus on visual and active exchanges. Many businesses don't benefit from making themselves highly visible and forcing

---

19 https://www.customerservicemanager.com/delivering-great-customer-service/
20 https://www.bankmycell.com/blog/why-millennials-ignore-calls#data

users to focus their attention on them. They benefit from creating automated electronic exchanges that are, for all practical purposes, invisible to the end user. Direct attention and engagement from end users should not always be a priority.

Consider Amazon, a paradigm of digital transformation if there ever was one. Although the company provides traditional customer service, that is not the reason for Amazon's unparalleled success. Its straightforward online transactions and innovative logistics make purchase, delivery, and returns simple, straightforward, and frictionless. The entire experience requires minimal customer effort. Younger generations that have grown up with this purchasing experience now expect other services to adhere to a similar standard. For better or worse, this is the comparison people unconsciously make regarding companies' business services.

Amazon's online store is far more efficient than typical B2B transactions in the electronics industry. Searching for parts, comparing them, and purchasing them is now expected to mirror Amazon's quality of service to qualify for "excellent customer experience." Of course, there are differences between a highly regulated, complex business process and a simple consumer purchase. In the former, aspects of communication must continue to follow established traditions of person-to-person conversation. But a large portion of communication within, and between, businesses is best kept in the background.

Personal communication will remain relevant and essential for novel business exchanges and processes that cannot be codified and reduced to a logical set of deterministic steps. But processes that can be made frictionless or invisible are much preferred. Adding customer service representatives will remain an option. Implementing technologies that attempt to emulate personal exchanges, such as automated telephone exchanges via interactive voice exchanges (IVR) or chatbots, will continue to provide cost savings. But automation that works in the background and eliminates tedious, time-consuming, repetitive activity will usually offer the best value.

Customer experience, including pain points, expectations, and business needs, is often a target for improvement during digital transformation. Quick reactions in this area involve polishing user interfaces or updating customer service representative scripts. But ideally, transformation is not restricted to these superficial actions and extends beyond technology additions or surface level upgrades to existing systems. It involves aligning the organization to support a better customer experience. This can require significant changes to internal processes, external processes, internal systems, and customer-facing systems. Effective solutions for better customer experience can be relatively nonintrusive and straightforward to implement.

Communication Participants

Internal vs. External Communication

Business functions like marketing, sales, and public relations support *external* customers, those outside the company. Digital technology has transformed these customers' habits. Companies that provide a seamless, consistent experience can cultivate "highly engaged customers" who are likely to return for additional business, reject competitors, and refer others to the organization. It is necessary to engage multiple departments in your organization with high-level support that effects changes in B2B transactions, customer service, sales, and marketing.

Keep in mind, that external business customers are simply consumers. They expect the same customer experience at work as they do at home. As noted above, they value ease and convenience when researching, comparing, and buying products in the corporate setting, just as they do on e-commerce sites.

Reducing unnecessary steps and streamlining cumbersome processes appeals to home consumers and B2B purchasers working under deadlines.

For companies to scale this effort, *internal* communication must also become a priority. Companies willing to invest in communication, keep employees informed, and provide accompanying resources are better positioned to respond in a coordinated manner to their external customers. This goes beyond traditional communication platforms and includes architecting data stores that minimize the access of stale or inaccurate data. Such data stores provide a canonical "source of truth" that streamlines decision-making, so seekers don't have to reconcile divergent sources of the same information.

In the context of digital transformation, internal parties need to understand *what* is changing and *why* it is changing. They also require communication from leadership regarding *how* they need to change to adapt to the new environment. One type of internal communication involves training: providing the skills that allow employees to excel at their jobs. This is a critical part of digital transformation. When companies fail to make a corresponding investment in building the skillset of their workforce, productivity gains are not realized.

B2B and End User Communication

Discussions related to communication strategies typically focus on individual end users. This is a highly challenging area because of diversity among users, complex coordination of channels required, and competition with many traditional and non-traditional competitors. But much in the electronics industry is oriented toward B2B exchanges. B2B transactions involve a smaller number of end users introducing a longer, drawn-out sales cycle with many different steps and participants along the way. Despite the fact that end users differ in the business world, B2B organizations need to employ similar strategies to appeal to individuals who are simply traditional consumers operating in a different space.

In many cases, end users do not want to talk to sales representatives during the early parts of their journey. They want to read marketing materials, watch videos, and access documentation independently, in a self-paced manner. They may want to tentatively interact by using social media to ask questions or by attending webinars. Digital transformation projects can use touch points to collect customer data throughout the process to better align marketing and sales efforts via analyses.

A comprehensive view of the customer journey highlights the need for cross-functional cooperation in providing an integrated, holistic customer experience. Marketing representatives supply materials accessed by users early in the customer journey, and sales representatives have conversations with them toward the end. While the sales team understands customer expectations and needs from direct conversations, marketing reps make observations based on how customers consume materials prior. Technical resources provide the underlying data stores and reports so decision-makers can take specific actions to improve the entire process.

Values of Communication

Again, the topic of communication—ordinary conversations and verbal exchanges—tends to be framed in personal, individualistic terms. Communicators emphasize qualities like "empathy" and "active listening." But in the overall interactions between two organizations, other factors are critical. Speed, accuracy, completeness, and clarity go a long way to satisfying needs on both sides to avoid confusion or irritation. Increasing meaningful information and reducing extraneous content are vital. The benefit of automation is that technology handles the bulk of straightforward transactions—often a larger amount of information than individuals could attain, which ensures higher quality communication overall.

Human relationships are multifaceted and complex. Simpler models can be helpful in limiting the scope of discussion and highlighting relevant aspects of communication that can be controlled.

Social exchange theory[21] reduces these costs and rewards, which drive relationship decisions. Costs include time, money, and effort. Rewards can be physical items, service results, or more intangible concerns such as acceptance or support. If a relationship is perceived as inequitable, alternatives are pursued. Additional factors impacting communication are the amount versus the magnitude of costs and rewards, time horizon (short-term vs. long-term benefits), autonomy, ambiguity, personal security, and social status of parties involved.

Analyzing a business process or customer service experience with costs and rewards in mind can be enlightening. There are often unnoticed costs involved that can be eliminated. Inefficient communication can be extremely costly in the perception of the end user. Reducing communication over several different channels to a single one can be valuable to this user. Reducing duplicate provisioning of information can also provide additional value. Removing interruptions of a communication exchange by introducing a different actor is a similar improvement. A benefit/reward that requires little or no action implies reduced cost. Quiet automation in the background is ideal for such exchanges that have little chance of producing enough direct rewards to justify the costs.

Communication Channels

Digital interactions can augment or replace repetitive, error-prone, and data-intensive human interactions. Still, they

---

21 https://en.wikipedia.org/wiki/Social_exchange_theory

cannot provide the same level of engagement, trust, and emotional connection. Face-to-face meetings and trade show interactions will remain helpful for the most personal engagements. Phone calls involve human voices and nuanced emotional content but can interrupt other activities. Paper mailings, brochures, and different types of physical advertising provide a tangible benefit with a visceral presence that cannot be matched virtually. The various qualitative differences should be understood so that they can be leveraged to provide the best end-user experience.

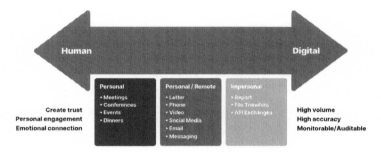

Communications over the internet have diverged beyond websites to cross-website communication via online advertising, social networking, messaging and chat applications, voice applications, and video conferencing. Built on internet technologies, this group of channels has significant potential in technical automation and augmentation.

API Communication

Two computers talking to each other does not qualify as human communication by strict definition. Still, when both computers are proxying for human counterparts, the practical result is absolutely communication and can be highly effective and profitable. Communication between two computers is accomplished using APIs which automate, or more accurately augment, communication between various parties involved in a business.

API communication has many practical benefits. Fewer manual steps taken by people to communicate a large amount of data will reduce mistakes and ensure consistent messaging. Exchanges can be routinely controlled and secure. The volume of information exchanged can be much larger than is possible in human interactions. The speed of communication is far faster than comparable communication by people. The direct digital transfer of data can reduce the number of parties involved and reduce the "whisper down the alley" effect where subtle transformations to data are introduced by personal exchanges. There is increased value when codifying communication previously involving multiple individuals is possible through a coherent grouping of API calls. Even with these immediate benefits aside, APIs are foundational to numerous technological initiatives.

Orbweaver Perspective: Customers

One of our customers observed:

"Being able to communicate information back and forth in seconds is really the 'wow' of this whole process...This response would have taken them weeks, with 5 to 10 times the amount of people that typically handle it."

Again, API communication will never completely eliminate communication by people. People need to manage APIs, data exchanges, and respond to these exchanges. People should be involved in downstream verification and addressing unusual requests/fallout. People need to identify changes in the marketplace or business context that require adjustments to API usage.

Technology and Terminology

While we will discuss specific technologies in greater detail in subsequent chapters, the basic mapping between human communication and digital technologies is straightforward.

Human Communication	Computer Analog
Message (spoken or written)	Unstructured data
Spreadsheets, Word docs	Semi-structured data
Multiple choice question-naires, paper forms	Structured data (XML, JSON)
Telephone call, mail	API using HTTP or higher-level protocol (SOAP, REST, RPC)
Filing cabinets	Digital storage (disk, cloud), databases

The mapping should assuage any concerns that digital technologies are inherently incapable of capturing human communication transactions. Though obvious, it is surprising how many businesses insist that a unique aspect of their business renders it disqualified for modernization. The straightforward mapping also should not be interpreted in strict terms that ignore the differences in communication mediums already mentioned, and the fact that an exchange that makes perfect sense between two people can be incredibly awkward when mapped naively to a digital solution.

Technologies to support groups of exchanges include workflow engines and orchestration systems. These can accommodate synchronous and asynchronous messaging, parallel processing, complex dependencies, and the like. Even when technologies are not explicitly used, business processes are encoded in workflows built into digital tooling.

Digital Solutions for Personal Benefits

The personal aspect of digital transformation redefines access and interactions employees have with consumers, clients, and fellow employees. It realigns communication to increase the value of interactions and eliminates ineffective exchanges and the resulting confusion. It results in better data capture, which improves business responsiveness. It ultimately provides benefits that are realized by people both within and outside the organization.

And as always, the transitions in this area are incremental and ongoing. Meaningful improvement is impossible even without solving every problem. Communication has always been, and will remain, a challenge. Digital transformation provides a set of tools and technologies that can eliminate many common issues and improve the business environment for all participants.

5

Business Processes

The electronics sector comprises various industries, including telecommunications, electronic components, industrial electronics, and consumer electronics. Despite differences among the businesses involved, a common landscape must be negotiated by all participants and specific aspects of digital technology relevant to all companies involved. This chapter addresses common considerations for business functions that are digital transformation candidates.

Electronic parts manufacturing directly impacts the production of common household items such as computers, mobile devices, televisions, and industrial and professional equipment. Nearly all technological advances in the modern economy depend on manufactured electronic components. The ubiquitous dependence on electronic components has resulted in established patterns of doing business within the industry. Each step in the process can benefit from leveraging digital technology oriented toward improving and optimizing the work involved.

Parts Search

A prerequisite to the broader parts procurement process is finding potential part candidates. Standard consumer public parts searches are of limited value, as they do not address concerns like bulk orders, parts packaging, quality metrics, or geographic and legal constraints. A sophisticated purchaser is aware of nomenclature embedded in segments of part numbers and won't restrict himself/herself to searching for an entire part number. The very idea of a part number is somewhat fluid, as there are both manufacturer part numbers and different designations used by suppliers and distributors. These topics don't even touch upon variations that depend on the buyer's corporate affiliation.

The complex and specialized requirements for buyers searching for parts have hindered the development of any single purpose entity for locating components. But part data, like any other type of data, has patterns and characteristics that allow it to be organized, sorted, filtered, and aggregated in ways that enable the people seeking parts to locate and procure them more effectively. In practice today, finding parts involves a combination of phone calls, spreadsheet references, and general-purpose internet searches.

Parts Procurement

The first step of the electronics manufacturing process proper is assembling a bill of materials (BOM). Manufacturers assemble BOMs to determine the materials needed for the project and their total cost. In the simplest case, this involves searching for parts in a paper or digital catalog and determining the associated prices.

At industrial scale, the process of assembling a BOM is broken out into a series of steps that involve iterative communication and competitive bidding by several suppliers. Determining the cost of parts is generally complex. It involves adjustments due to agreements between customers and suppliers, availability of substitute products, pricing based on quantity purchased, and other considerations. Multiple parties, including representatives from purchasing, accounting, sales, and finance, might contribute or provide sign-off. Despite these intricacies, the number of people involved, and the total interactions required, the final result is essentially the same as the simple case: a list of parts and prices.

Steps related to assembling a BOM and procuring parts have converged on a set of well-defined processes despite competition and secrecy within the industry. Contract manufacturers (CMs) generally construct the BOM (and associate prices) through a series of exchanges referred to as the request for quote (RFQ) process. This allows potential suppliers to competitively cost the parts ultimately selected. Depending on the nature and complexity of the project, several procurement communications may precede the RFQ. Examples include a request for information (RFI) or request for proposal (RFP).

A sequence diagram describes an ordered set of interactions between multiple objects, typically people or software systems. Diagrams of this type can be used by software developers and business professionals to understand requirements for a new system or to document an existing process. Modeling object interactions is a core task performed during system analysis and design. Business processes in the electronics industry can be challenging to understand, but a visualization of this type can go a long way toward helping interested parties understand what is involved and what process adjustments can be made.

Note that a sequence diagram is but one of many ways to represent business processes. Flow charts can also be useful, but don't contain the temporal ordering evident in a sequence diagram. Business process modeling (BPM) software can also be used to capture and represent business processes, and even provide a platform for implementing automation. Regardless of the visualization method, it is important to concisely express cross-functional activities that comprise a business process. This will promote the clear communication and buy-in required to successfully enact digital transformation across the organization.

The following sequence diagram describes one possible example of the high-level activities involved in the overall procurement process. Four parties (or "actors") are represented—three within a company making a purchase and one external supplier.

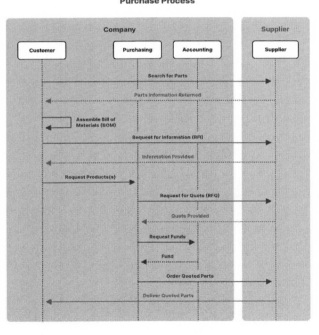

Purchase Process

Remember, this is a high-level sequence diagram; a single interaction such as "search for parts" might involve *multiple* suppliers, searching through *several* online sources, disparate spreadsheets, and paper catalogs. It likely includes other standard business documents like purchase orders and invoices.

In a larger scale project, it makes sense to decompose a high-level sequence diagram into a series of lower-level diagrams to capture all relevant information adequately. This level of visualization is sufficient to represent commonalities among various parts of the electronics industry.

The activities and interactions represented above are candidates for software automation. For example:

- A web application with a search engine containing supplier data can be used to search for parts and retrieve related information. The actual data is stored in a database. This search engine may be run by the supplier or a third party that maintains data for multiple suppliers. The value of a "digital transformation" at this isolated point is to consolidate disparate data sources, normalize the data to follow consistent conventions, ensure the data is timely, and make data retrieval quick.

- A BOM construction utility enables the creation of a bill of materials quickly, accurately, and efficiently. Spreadsheets are flexible and can easily accommodate part, quantity, and price data. Plug-ins can provide additional validation or integration with another system or platform. There are also dedicated desktop and online tools for creating and sending BOMs to various participants in the procurement process. Automation in this area ensures fast, accurate, auditable construction and communication of BOMs for all interested parties.

- Subsequent steps represented in the diagram can be similarly implemented as independent web applications (or features of existing ones) where customers make requests of suppliers. For instance, the RFI interaction between the customer and supplier is a straightforward exchange. It can be formalized as a form in the web application already described that hosts the parts search engine.

• Combining the parts search engine and RFI interaction highlights the separate, standalone BOM construction utility. This, too, could be integrated with the web application that includes the RFI interaction and parts search. It might also involve BOM plug-in integration with an API exposed by the web application. Progressing along this line of thinking, it is apparent that customer/supplier interactions can be organized to utilize a unified application platform.

• The purchasing and accounting interactions are likely recorded in an Enterprise Resource Planning (ERP) system. Rather than using isolated systems or email messages to communicate with these interactions, APIs can be constructed to automate the exchanges. Business users involved in purchasing, accounts, and supplier sales can still be involved, but their work will likely involve validation of automatically generated order activities and addressing orders that are unusual or outside the scope of system design.

Layers of essential undergirding technologies serve as dependencies required to build advanced, industry-specific solutions. Databases, search engines, web applications, and APIs aren't the latest media darlings in the technology world, but they are foundational as the underlying infrastructure to support any other subsequent modern technology choice. For instance, a large amount of clean, reliable, timely data is required for technologies that more directly guide strategic decision-making for the organization. Thus, databases, including traditional relational databases, serve an absolutely essential role for such projects.

Advanced Value-Added Systems

Artificial Intelligence (AI) is a broad term used to describe software that performs tasks normally handled by humans and requires some capability that appears "intelligent" when viewed from the outside. Machine learning (ML) and neural networks have received a great deal of attention in recent years, especially in the field of computer vision. ML can be used for classification activities, such as categorizing purchasing transactions into categories or matching invoices with vendors. Regression activities make it possible to predict a continuous value, such as the number of days until a part becomes available.

Forecasting: Time series forecasting activities sometimes use ML algorithms, but often can be performed using techniques that separate the "signal" from seasons and trends influencing a time series (e.g., ARIMA or AutoRegressive Integrated Moving Average). These can be used to make predictions about upcoming purchasing activity.

APIs are required to serve as the communication points and define the content of transactions across remote networks. As such, they are foundational for applications that imitate human language interactions or those that allow sensory input from the physical world.

Chatbots and **Interactive Voice Response** applications have become popular for augmenting human customer service representatives. In both cases, such systems frequently need to retrieve data from a remote system much the way a human customer service representative would do using a website. APIs provide the connectivity and raw data used by these applications to guide their responses. In some cases, natural language processing (NLP) techniques assist in crafting responses, many of which require data if based on ML techniques. Software that augments customer service activities clearly fits into many parts of the procurement process.

Internet of things (IoT) devices communicate with other devices and software over the internet or other networks. Again, APIs are needed to provide the messaging and communication services between participating systems. Sensors can be used in inventory management to track parts as they are shipped and for other purposes surrounding procurement.

Blockchain could replace traditional databases for some functions. But blockchains are fundamentally a means for storing data--simple distributed ledgers. They must be interacted with via an interface of some sort. Depending on the implementation, this might be a web API. In any case, web APIs would remain involved in other parts of the procurement process and would call the blockchain, rather than databases, to perform transactions. A group of participants buying and selling parts could disintermediate businesses serving as "middle men" trusted to arbitrate transactions between parties and moderate their activities.

Many lower-level details are involved in a full implementation to digitize a procurement process, but the broad picture is clear. Digital transformation of the interactions via automation and integration software can accommodate many standard purchasing transactions – in your company or those of your competitors. Establishing a firm foundation built on databases, web applications, and APIs allows subsequent advancements to be added as needed.

Orbweaver Perspective: Platform

CTO Tony Powell stated: "The RFQ process is vital to the supplier-client relationship. Many organizations have retained manual RFQ processes, which are a burden, especially for companies in the electronics manufacturing industry. Distributors, manufacturers, and suppliers waste thousands of hours and millions of dollars tackling orders and requests because of outdated, inefficient processes.

Thankfully, it is possible to eliminate these pain points with the application of intelligent and strategic RFQ management tools. By automating the RFQ process, any aspect of the procurement cycle can be streamlined, providing speed, efficiency, and transparency to all parties throughout the entire process.

• *Building the Product*

Parts procurement is only the first in a sequence of steps involved in the manufacturing of a final product. The BOM serves as input for the design process where blueprints are created. The product is prototyped, tested, and verified for consumer use, with quality and speed being of utmost importance. Both internal and external parties can be identified and represented as actors in a sequence diagram similar to the one shown above. Stakeholder interactions reveal areas where digital transformation efforts can provide a competitive edge in quickly creating high quality products.

By definition, scaling up production is an automation and optimization effort. The focus typically is on reducing set-up costs and decreasing throughput times. Final product distribution brings the product into the physical world via transport and logistics. There are opportunities for digital transformation throughout this effort. Following production, customer communication, repairs, returns, and maintenance activities entail well-defined, effectively choreographed exchanges among parties.

Despite the product build being independent of parts procurement, there is a clear connection regarding overall business objectives stemming from critical functions. At a minimum, financial reporting will be used to reconcile costs of raw materials and sales of the end product to determine profitability. Other connections may be beneficial earlier in the process; for instance, those involved in production could use updates about procurement status to more efficiently schedule work. These types of connections, which inevitable arise informally, may be "low-hanging fruit" for digital transformation efforts that bridge communications and automatically update interested parties with relevant information.

Inventory Management

Electronic companies balance two objectives that are at odds: short delivery times and minimum capital tied up in inventory. Inventory management can exist at multiple levels as suppliers of a component rely on upstream component suppliers to manufacture a product they supply.

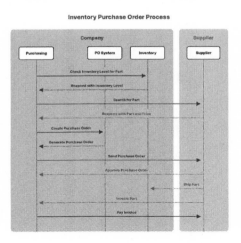

Orbweaver Perspective: Platform

The line of thinking referenced above also shows the trajectory Orbweaver has pursued in building out our platform over time. Interacting with electronics industry participants and automating their internal exchanges and interactions with one another has convinced us of the potential for a consistent platform where industry participants do business in a far more efficient and cost-effective manner. Our focus on technical solutions and common business patterns frees our customers to focus on their core business concerns while gaining state-of-theart digital transformation solutions.

This high-level diagram captures fairly common aspects of this type of business process. Three of the actors are presumably human participants: representatives from purchasing, inventory, and the external supplier. One actor is a system--a piece of software used to record and generate purchase orders that are then sent for approval by the purchasing department to the supplier. Actors are an abstract concept and are more commonly referred to as "entities." They can therefore represent anything that acts in a system: a single individual, a collective group of individuals, a discrete department or organization, a software system, etc. The important concern is that actors must be represented to the degree that all sequential interactions are adequately captured.

Like the previous diagram, interactions in this high-level illustration could be decomposed to allow you to effectively "drill down" to a greater level of detail. For example, the creation of the purchase order could involve input and approval from several parties. Each could be represented in this diagram to describe the details. This type of analysis is essential when attempting to build a digital solution that comprehensively represents and replaces previously manual processes.

Distribution and Supply Chain Concerns

The electronic parts supply chain is an immensely complex logistical construct. A variety of companies located in various geographical regions manufactures parts. Disruptions can arise unexpectedly and have cascading effects on downstream participants. Attempts to mitigate such disruptions are built into the procurement process. For example, the parts in a BOM might have viable substitutes. Ideally, companies have adequate visibility into the status of distribution pipelines and the supply chain as a whole to manage production and adjust plans as needed. Digital transformation projects can be used to increase visibility into portions of the supply chain and provide smooth, frictionless interactions to respond to changes. Consider the alternate part approval process shown below.

Alternate Part Approval

It's easy to imagine individuals in each department handling this process by either using spreadsheets and email. But consider a company that automates the referenced system, allowing a purchaser to immediately view parts available from several suppliers. Engineering could provide lists of pre-approved parts that are instantly substituted as needed, based on availability. The purchaser could submit the form and order the parts immediately from a supplier. If required, the purchaser's submission could be added to a queue of orders to be approved by engineering using the same web application. The result is a clear, auditable process that eliminates the possibility of errors and miscommunications common in a series of protracted human conversations.

Technology and Business Processes
Databases

Relational databases store data in a structured format. Tables have a defined list of columns, and columns are assigned a distinct data type (character string, number, integer, decimal, date, etc.). Additional constraints can further specify the data stored in the databases and the relationships between the tables. This restrictive structuring provides several benefits. Consistently stored, normalized data is far easier to summarize and process.

In addition, relational databases support transactions. The acronym ACID refers to four key properties of a transaction: atomicity, consistency, isolation, and durability. These properties provide guarantees regarding data validity despite errors, power failures, and other problems. Databases can capture all changes made over time through vendor-specific features such as auditing and system versioning (or through custom solutions using triggers or stored procedures). The combination of structured data and database transactions ensures that data is stored and managed in a clear way, data loss is minimized, and that data can be changed in a controlled manner.

Orbweaver Perspective: Platform

RFQ management tools. By automating the RFQ process, any aspect of the procurement cycle can be streamlined, providing speed, efficiency, and transparency to all parties throughout the entire process."

NoSQL solutions have received a great deal of attention in recent years. NoSQL databases are increasingly used in big data and real-time web applications. These databases typically rely upon different storage and data representation methods. They might be classified as a key-value store, document store, graph database, object database, or hybrid. Some are related to distributed and parallel processing ecosystems, such as Apache Hadoop. Others are simply caches or primitive object stores that have grown into more full-fledged services.

NoSQL databases flourish in situations where a very specific problem is being solved at scale. Their initial design was inspired by a need to overcome a specific limitation in relational databases. In most cases, the data needed to be processed at a high velocity, consumed at a high volume, or have a specific structure for representing or storing data.

When adopting a NoSQL database, it is easy to focus on the selling point to the exclusion of limitations that are not evident at first glance. NoSQL databases have been implemented in many situations that provide limited, if any, benefit and incur significant technical debt. Reasons for this assertion are as follows:

Definition of big data: The perception of what qualifies as big can be confusing. Very few business problems actually deal with truly big data. Modern relational databases on properly sized hardware can handle an astounding amount of data. For example, Excel spreadsheets in 64-bit environments are limited only by available memory and system resources.[22] SQLite, a widely used relational database that stores its data in a single file capable of running on a desktop machine, can hold up to 281 TB of data.[23] Numbers this big used to only be discussed in the scientific realm. Modern computer hardware storage and processing can handle quantities of data that were previously inconceivable.

Need for parallel processing: If you want to do work quicker, one simple way is to have more workers. Data sets can be split up among processes that work in parallel and significantly reduce the time required. This is undeniable in isolation but is not always understood in the context of the broader business process. Optimization efforts implemented without clear measures tend to optimize the wrong tasks. Faster is better, but if you make a 100x performance improvement to processing in a business process where the major bottleneck is the response time of an external vendor, the gain is minimal or meaningless.

The myth of no ETL: NoSQL databases and data lakes, in general, are often presented as a solution to eliminating Extract-Transform-Load (ETL) operations required by traditional databases and data warehouses. The flip side is that unstructured data that needs to be cleaned up and transformed for reporting and analytics tends not to be emphasized. In fact, restricting data during import is much more straightforward than trying to identify, validate, and clean data before using it to derive actionable information. Without a great deal of management and oversight, data lakes degrade into data swamps. Any savings from eliminating ETL is lost when the final result is expensive, low-quality reporting and analytics.

---

22 https://support.microsoft.com/en-us/office/data-model-specifica-tion-and-limits-19aa79f8-e6e8-45a8-9be2-b58778fd68ef

23 https://www.sqlite.org/limits.html

Challenges with querying: Along with the variation in storage and data structure representation with NoSQL databases comes a wide variety of software development kits (SDKs), querying languages, and interfaces for executing queries. Ironically, many NoSQL products add a SQL-like language to their solution because of its popularity. These work well enough under the proper conditions. However, a subtle challenge is missed by those who have not worked through database projects from initiation to production. A common occurrence in a relational database project is identifying a query late in the game that is needed for reporting. This query may need to be tuned and indexes added to support needed performance. Otherwise, this late requirement can be easily accommodated. This is not always the case in the NoSQL world. In some cases, the patterns for querying must be understood up front to store the data in a way capable of being queried. This is not a limitation one wants to find late in a project schedule.

Transactions for distributed storage trade-off: Programmers take for granted ACID storage guarantees offered by relational databases. Some NoSQL solutions remove ACID transactions which allow blisteringly fast inserts of new data and enables the store of the data over multiple machines in a distributed cluster, to ensure availability should a node in the cluster crash. The benefits are apparent, but the lack of ACID transactions means an attempt to read the data inserted and immediately re-queried might unexpectedly not be found.

NoSQL databases can be an extremely useful solution to very specific, well understood problems. They are designed to tackle specific types of challenges far better than a typical relational database system. However, they require a defined architectural usage and management to provide benefit in the areas where they are a good fit.

User Interfaces

Digital systems exist to support human needs and always include human involvement. Full and unsupervised automation is rarely a business goal. When it is, the problem is either trivial or not well understood. Humans are highly versatile and adaptive to new information and changes in an environment. Software systems are not. In addition, legal and ethical concerns persist regarding human ownership and responsibility over given domains that require intervention in an otherwise automated process. The goal of digital transformation is the augmentation of processes, not the elimination of human involvement. As such, user experience (UX) and user interface (UI) design are important factors when automating business processes. An easily understandable, efficient, and clear process will find willing human participants. One that is confusing, cumbersome, and of unclear value to the end user will be worked around or avoided. Examples of UIs include web applications, mobile devices, desktop applications, and voice applications.

APIs

A key aspect of transforming remote communication expressed in sequence diagrams is replacing phone calls, text messages, and email with APIs. Ideally, legacy file transfers are similarly integrated so that data is not simply moved, but also extracted, from one system and ingested by another automatically. An automated data transfer that eliminates human intervention also has advantages from a data governance and compliance perspective.

APIs, the interfaces that allow various systems to communicate, provide a foundation for subsequent technological growth. While they are the access points for data throughout the organization, they also open up the possibility of communication outside the organization. APIs running on an intranet (or the internet) enable data flow and transactions between systems that are otherwise in isolated silos.

APIs that communicate data between systems have layers of built-in features to eliminate communication errors. One example is the use of well-formed, valid XML for communications as used in legacy SOAP applications and modern REST APIs. If a document is well-formed, it meets the basic W3C standards required to qualify as XML. If a document were cut off mid-creation or mangled, the document would be rejected, and no further processing would occur. An additional layer of validation is available by defining a schema that describes the content of the XML document in greater detail, for instance, by ensuring that a given, well-formed XML document contains a properly formatted order number, shipping address, and order date. XML documents that have valid type information according to the associated schema are said to be valid. These are only a few of many possible validation options, and similar alternatives exist for other formats, like JSON.

The standardization involved in creating an API results in highly regular data that matches expected data types and categories. This makes the data far easier to summarize, report on, and use for forecasting or predictive analysis initiatives. The humble API is a workhorse technology that provides immense technical and business benefits when strategically placed into portions of the business that are prime candidates for automation.

Workflow Engines

Humans define patterns of work that gradually mature and coalesce into a standard set of steps as a workflow. Digital transformation embeds some or all of a workflow into a series of transactions between participating systems using APIs. Many systems contain ad-hoc workflow processing embedded in their design. Ad-hoc workflows can be further abstracted into externalized configurable assets, allowing for higher adaptability. This has led to the development of general-purpose workflow engines.

Workflow engines like Apache Airflow[24] are platforms for running directed acyclic graphs (DAGs) of tasks. These provide a formal model for workflows conducive to the constraints required by many types of scheduling and processing tasks. A DAG consists of vertices and edges. Each edge is directed from one vertex to another. These edges can be followed in order and never form a closed loop. Generalpurpose workflow engines provide a powerful method of implementing many types of everyday workflows. But the mathematical rigor and nomenclature used in such systems can be confusing and are generally handled by professional software developers. For example, Airflow allows Python script to be defined, which serves as a configuration file specifying a DAG's structure as code.

Some workflow systems target business users rather than software developers. Activiti[25] and Flowable[26] attempt to make workflows more accessible to business users via Business Process Modeling Notation (BPMN). BPMN is a graphical notation that depicts the steps in a business process. The allure of these sorts of projects is that they provide an extensible, flexible means of defining arbitrary business processes. These systems are very good at simple workflows consisting of a task or two, but require software developer support to implement advanced features and complex workflows.

Special purpose SaaS systems have emerged as a truly business-friendly way of providing enterprise workflow support without involving software developers directly.

---

24 https://github.com/apache/incubator-airflow

25 https://www.activiti.org/

26 https://github.com/flowable/flowable-engine

Artificial Intelligence and Machine Learning

Machine learning (ML) is one technique in AI that has been popular in recent years. In essence, rather than having a developer write a program to categorize an input or predict a value, data is organized and used to automatically create a model that can be used to produce a similar result – in some cases with greater accuracy than the programmer can provide. For example, a programmer could write a program that "looks at" an image of an electronic part, records characteristics about the image, and, based on the logic used to analyze those characteristics, provides an output indicating whether it is a capacitor, a transistor, or an inductor. This type of challenging task would require a great deal of effort on the part of a programmer. Computer vision takes advantage of ML models to allow a model to be built to perform the same task. The caveat is that a large number of labeled images needs to be used as input to train the model.

ML models require a vast amount of data. If the data is not stored in a consistent manner in a database, it will not be usable. If it is in a database, the data must be exported and normalized. If relevant data resides in multiple locations, APIs might play a part in assembling a data set used to train a model. Again, fundamental technologies are foundational for the adoption of more recent cutting-edge innovations.

Conclusion

The electronics industry has established certain patterns of doing business. Although there is significant variation in each company, all participating members of the industry, as a whole, can benefit from the adoption of technology to set the stage for transformational success and overcoming business challenges in the future. This chapter introduced the significant concerns related to digital transformation that all competitive companies are addressing, as well as the primary technologies they have begun to adopt.

6

Implementation: Transforming Your Business

Strategy-informed ambition sparks the initiation of a project that can ultimately transform a business. There is no one-size-fits-all solution for enacting change in the form of digital transformation or any other realm. Every organization has its own culture, cadence, and capabilities. Project budgeting and costs vary. The risk tolerance, scope, and expectations are never standard. That said, there is a general shape or framework for digital transformation. It can be understood by thinking through the project from strategic, tactical, and operational levels. Various activities are addressed at each level and map to other activities within the level and at adjacent levels. This is not a strict project plan, but rather a framework that can be used to ensure project activities are accurately representing areas of need.

Strategic Review

The strategic review involves defining the overall plan of action regarding the project. A relatively small number of core

Orbweaver Perspective: Platform

Workflows in the electronic industry are identifiable, but deceptively complex. Orbweaver's product line includes support for API integration and orchestration,1 along with workflows to make your data available and transparent across multiple departments.2 Support for all of the standard workflows in use in contract manufacturing are available. Quoting, purchasing, forecasting, invoicing, and revising demands all can be organized across business units into single workstreams that are unified in format, performance monitoring, and permissions across an organization. As an online portal, it can be accessed anywhere in the world at all times.

---

1 https://www.orbweaver.com/products/datahub/

2 https://www.orbweaver.com/products/advance/

project owners generate high-level ideas. In broad strokes, questions that should be answered include:

- What is the goal of the project?

- What needs to be changed (and why)?

- Who is involved in making the change (both chief stakeholders and peripheral participants)?

- How will the status and overall success of the project be measured?

Goals for the project should be aligned with overall organizational goals. Nuances of perspective can inform your path forward, regardless of organizational goals. A company goal might be to become the eading manufacturer of a specific line of electronic components. This goal might be recast or measured with an eye toward customer focus if pivotal for a given project. The goal, then, is revised, so the company becomes the leading manufacturer of a specific line of electronic components.

Tactical Planning

At this point, managers of the "doers" get involved. Management breaks down project goals into specific measurable subprojects (or objectives). Management evaluates the current systems and workflows in use. These decision-makers identify the partners and employees responsible for doing the work and use metrics selected during strategic planning to derive baseline values that will be used in subsequent evaluations.

It is difficult to overemphasize the importance of ensuring all participants are involved and that interests are aligned. A perfectly implemented system can be left unused if a faulty, yet familiar, way of performing the work remains available to an unwilling or unincentivized workforce. In addition, the data and information required to implement improvements rely on the efforts of those performing day-to-day operations. Relatively high-level buy-in and involvement are nonnegotiable for large scale efforts that span multiple managers in a given company.

Operational Implementation

This stage entails putting the tactical plans into action: implementing system development, upgrades, and integration efforts. Training is designed and implemented with participants in revised workflows. As systems reach operability, metrics are collected to determine the impact of the changes and whether or not further changes are required. The schedule should incorporate small iterations and tight feedback loops with measurable and defined objectives. Adjustments will be needed over time, so, whenever possible, changes should be made to maximize the visibilityof both the changes themselves and the processes that have been affected by the change.

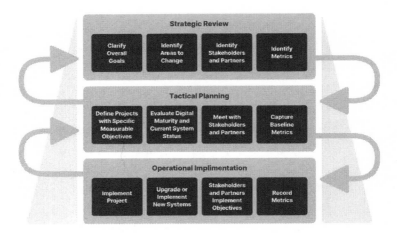

Iterations and Revisions

Agile methodologies have gained popularity based on the recognition that so-called "waterfall" methods fail due to ill-advised attempts to foresee every possible project contingency. The arrows on the sides of the diagram above reflect the recognition that rather than proceeding in a straightforward, linear fashion regardless of the situation, it is necessary to step back, revisit plans, and make revisions based on information discovery. Remember, workflows in the electronics industry are highly sophisticated and change over time, making their revision and automation complex. High-level management is often unaware of the many significant details in this domain. As such, new requirements must be codified and fed back into the plan over time to ensure the best possible transformation results.

The project's tactical and operational aspects are, by necessity, lower-level and more specific and individualized to each project. On the other hand, the strategic level is more abstract and must be considered generally to enable insights for all organizations participating in a digital transformation initiative.

Strategic Organization Evaluation

There are many elements to consider within an organization when working through digital transformational planning. The business strategy and value proposition of the company undergird any changes enacted. The current and future customer base and corresponding marketing infrastructure are affected both directly and indirectly by the project. The composition and skill set of operations staff and support structure provide guidelines and constraints for strategy. And, of course, the current systems and technology in use provide a foundation on which subsequent changes can be built.

Organizational Maturity

There are numerous "maturity models" that help provide a comprehensive framework for categorizing activities and identifying areas to investigate when planning. These types of models are inevitably implemented into a project management framework that seeks to start with high-level representations of the state of the organization, then proceed to map specific tasks and interventions aimed at improving the organization. The focus of this section is not the wholesale adoption of any given approach, but rather the provision of a frame of reference at a strategic level to guide decisions regarding digital transformation initiatives and technological options.

Capability Maturity Model

The Capability Maturity Model,[27] dating back to 1986, is based on data collected from organizations that contracted with the U.S. Department of Defense. The focus of maturity in this context is formality and optimization of processes.

---

27 https://en.wikipedia.org/wiki/Capability_Maturity_Model

Less mature organizations rely primarily on individual effort and are not process driven. More mature organizations are resilient and efficient, less reliant on specific individuals, and more on well-managed, standardized, measurable business processes progressively improved and optimized over time.

Level	Description
Initial	Reliant on individual (heroic) effort
Repeatable	Documented steps to process
Defined	Delineated as a standard business process
Capable	Quantitative management of process using metrics
Efficient	Standard metrics across projects, optimization, and improvement

Small entrepreneurial organizations inevitably start low on the scale, but their successful growth depends on maturing to subsequent levels. Likewise, large companies often have matured in certain business areas, but there are opportunities to improve areas of the business that are newer, recently disrupted, or facing other types of change.

Data and Analytics Maturity Index

One example is based on a study by Keystone Strategy (2016).[28] The company designed a data and analytics maturity index consisting of four stages:

Stage	Name	Data Platform	Data Usage
1	Reactive	Local structured data	Reactive
2	Informative	Centralized monitored structured data	Managed

3	Predictive	Comprehensive data with business intelligence (BI)	Systematic analysis / predictive modeling
4	Transformative	Transformational data platform	Drive business, create new value

Each of the stages can be considered as they relate to data platform products:

Product
Operational databases
Enterprise data warehouse (EDW)
Business intelligence (BI)
Advanced analytics
Enterprise data lake (EDL)
Cloud computing infrastructure

The study, which was sponsored by Microsoft, has value in providing a framework for considering functional areas and an organization's ability to take tangible actions based on its data. The dated study concludes that maturity can be attained by adopting the latest, greatest technologies and ensuring they are available for use. Nevertheless, it is worth considering how capable your organization is of using its available data and analytics for decision-making. Further, evaluation does involve considering the stage of maturity and products, as well as platforms (or equivalent services) in use.

Digital transformation today is targeted, considering specific business operations, functions, and pain points to address, as opposed to blind adoption of new technology. Note that the product categories listed above can be replaced with SaaS platforms and services. The goal of digital transformation is not simply the uncritical adoption of "better" or "faster" technology across the board. It requires specific business understanding and operational knowledge. It targets initiatives that incorporate automation and data management in a focused manner, aligned with defined business goals to deliver targeted, measurable value.

Data-driven Marketing Maturity

Research[29] from the Boston Consulting Group (BCG) commissioned by Google specified four stages of data-driven marketing maturity. This framework can broadly be applied outside marketing applications by considering business processes involving internal customers. The focus is less on marketing itself and more on the progression of improving data-driven decision making and interdepartmental collaboration.

Stage	*Analogy*	*Description*
Nascent	Crawling	The company doesn't trust relying on data. Little departmental collaboration.
Emerging	Walking	Comfortable collecting/using data. Process improvements. Some collaboration.
Connected	Running	Data-driven business practices across multiple departments and channels.

---

29 https://marketingplatform.google.com/about/resources/ bcg-delivering-meaningful-moments/

Multi-moment	Flying	Digital transformation focused on individual customer transactions. Able to pursue efficiencies across channels.

Additional models look closer at the customer, company strategy, technology, operations, and other aspects of the organization. Metrics can be defined on each front. For instance, an organization can create customer-specific metrics to measure engagement, quality of experience, observed behavior, and subjective brand perception. Technology metrics are often available via scanning tools and automated processes. Change management, resource management, standards, and governance are considerations when assessing project success. And lest the focus is lost, the company's value proposition should always be at the core of decision-making.

Project Management

Several considerations involved in software engagements inform this chapter.[30] The first of these pertains to "drawing the blueprints" for the project based on the types of assessments described earlier. It is also important to involve a project champion and to establish (and work within) a budget. These considerations set the stage for executing the plans and promoting the adoption of the new system and business processes.

Framework

Depending on your organization's size and the endeavor's scale, a large-scale, rigorous approach might be warranted. But rather than endlessly obsess over details of organizational process, it is better to engage and actively implement a

---

30 https://www.orbweaver.com/the-orbweaver-process-of-engagement/

time-boxed, well-defined initiative targeted at a specific goal. A great deal can be learned by implementing a digital project that will provide feedback for subsequent projects. Models and metrics can take on a life of their own if not filtered and shaped by proper managerial guidance.

Abstract models are instrumental in understanding a project relative to the overall organization or in comparison to other projects. It's hard to visualize this kind of information without a reasonable model. But left unchecked, model creation and organizational assessment can become an end unto themselves. In our experience, management is well aware of the status of their organization through years of experience. Models provide an organizational framework for discussion and initial project selection. Project initiation results in feedback from the business itself, which is vital for shaping an effective, comprehensive digital transformation strategy over time.

Project Champions

Significant change requires groups of people. But people seldom self-organize effectively on a large scale without leadership. Select individuals must provide oversight, not simply through management, but through leadership. Leadership involves experienced, motivated, and energetic communication. At the helm of a project, this team member is a project champion. Leaders ensure all parties are aligned and advancing to complete the project successfully. Leaders in business transformation consistently articulate the value achievable through transformation, and monitor, measure, and track progress throughout the project's life.

Organizational transformation is primarily accomplished by running well-defined projects. Other methods might be more straightforward and require less coordination, but they are not as successful in effecting change. Improvement is not realized through unreflective cost cutting. Creative but short-sighted initiatives that involve little-to-no cost or leadership engagement typically yield few results, and also frustrate good employees. Experienced employees want to apply their knowledge to clearly defined, achievable expectations. This requires a budgeted project with clearly defined leadership.

A project champion is a coach with organizational credibility, industry knowledge, and, ideally, a methodology aligned with the vision for improvements. He or she gathers the required stakeholders, monitors schedules and milestone deliverables, and inspires and supports team members along the way. When partnering with outside organizations, a project champion is even more essential in the role of primary conduit for information flowing to and from the vendor.

Favorably, if a digital transformation is considered advantageous to all participants, changes are easy to implement. Change generally requires some people to work differently, spend differently, or interact with different people in a new way. Still, even changes that demonstrably meet company goals, like improving value, enabling cost savings, and improving customer satisfaction, will be resisted by those on whom change has been forced. The project champion can overcome much of this resistance by carefully planning and clearly articulating the value to all participants in the process.

Orbweaver Perspective: Platform

The "champion with authority" should be a single point of contact who has the vision and authority to drive the project through all phases to completion. This is often the person responsible for improving the organization, not necessarily a person who will use the product on a daily basis (though his input is critical!).

Budget

Change comes at a cost. Building and configuring software, training staff, and creating and evaluating metrics takes time and resources. Misguided attempts to enact substantial change "on the cheap" generally result in dubious results and technical debt. Technical debt means the organization must incur costs at a later point to fix, improve, modernize, or adapt a suboptimal solution.

While costs are inevitable, they should not be left unchecked. Project constraints related to budgeting help guide solutions to be both effective and sustainable. In many cases, digital transformation can result in considerable cost savings. The path to this savings requires the output of initial expenses, experimentation, and plan revision before the solution is in place.

Execution

As anyone in business can attest, many meetings include long, detailed, compelling conversations that conclude without specific actionable items. Clear responsibility for defined, achievable tasks is an absolute requirement if those conversations are to translate into organizational action. A project champion with a defined budget is in an optimal position to host meetings that will result in increased productivity for the organization.

Execution must be broken up into defined steps and deliverables. These milestones serve as checkpoints where project team members demonstrate task completion and measurable progress. Completion of one milestone is a prerequisite for proceeding to the next. Deliverables must be validated and approved as complying with the quantifiable results previously defined. Projects properly mapped to smaller incremental improvements begin to pay dividends before the overall project is completed. It is essential to have distinct, well-defined steps in a project to realize these benefits.

That said, keeping the overarching project goals in mind is important. It is necessary from time to time to step back and look at the big picture. The real value of any significant digital transformation emerges over time through sustainable, adaptable modifications that endure. The right capabilities, competencies, and culture are required for sustaining and growing the value of the transformation in the long run.

Both automated and human management are critical as the project progresses. Communication between participants is ideally centralized and available as new parties enter the process. Software development should use a software development life cycle (SDLC) that includes change control, regulated deployment, and testing and evaluation by relevant parties. Active involvement during project execution will allow stakeholders to identify problems early and adjust proactively to avoid costly remediation.

> ### *Orbweaver Perspective: Project Execution*
>
> Once construction begins, team engagement is critical throughout the process. As with new home construction, the buyer is interested in progress and wants to stop by often. We expect the same: that you will "stop by often" to ensure things are going as agreed.
>
> Active participation involves answering questions, keeping internal stakeholders apprised, allocating resources to support the execution of the project, and communicating with the entire project team.
>
> With appropriate client engagement, the project will be executed perfectly.

Adoption

Metrics also should be available to objectively monitor project adoption. Typically, a relatively small group of project participants is intimately familiar with project progress, its rationale, and the extent and value of the changes being made. Despite attempts to educate, others who are directly impacted by the project are often unaware of this information. Sometimes, focusing on eads employees to knowingly or unknowingly filter out communication provided. Prior communication and training may need to be repackaged and adoption metrics evaluated after each iteration. Over time, the new process and system become "the job" for people in these positions. After this initial onboarding and education, ongoing adoption will take on a life of its own, requiring far less direct intervention and handholding.

Orbweaver Perspective: Project Adoption

Adoption and engaged use of the final product is vital to project success. Leading up to and following product launch, we encourage our clients to actively market the product internally, continually soliciting feedback and keeping stakeholders and users engaged. Their buy-in and ultimate satisfaction are critical to a successful outcome.

Just as it would be a shame to build a house that remained empty, it would likewise be disappointing for a new project rollout to go unused. In addition to the client's obligation to promote, communicate, and engage users and stakeholders, Orbweaver provides on-site tutorials, training, and continual support to help transition your company to the new software.

We highly encourage our clients to take advantage of these resources. It is ultimately a joint responsibility to ensure that the new product is not only rolled out successfully, but gains acceptance and wide adoption across the user team.

Celebration

Transformation today often takes place at an uncomfortably fast pace, requiring a high level of integration and alignment that taxes the resources of even the best organizations. Project completion requires the management of large amounts of information in compressed timeframes. Countless decisions must be made that affect many aspects of strategy and operations. Successful project completion demonstrates that disparate elements and parties have been aligned and can now achieve bold new goals, now and into the future.

The culmination of a project should be a positive event. Project management frequently looks at the end of a project with a neutral stance, both positive and negative outcomes along the way shaping the perspective. The meetings following implementation are sometimes specified using the rather macabre term "postmortem." Digital transformation involves enacting change to achieve positive outcomes for people inside and outside of a business. Anyone can find things to criticize. Challenges are part of the process, and improvements can be made in the future. Good leadership recognizes the effort and diligence required throughout the project and celebrates the victories.

Adopting transformative automated software solutions to solve everyday pain points should be recognized by all involved. After a successful launch, it is well worth acknowledging the accomplishment and enjoying this exciting time.

7

Automation for Integration

A Necessary Progression

Recall the diagram shown in chapter 1 that represents stages in digital transformation. The diagram shows that digital transformation can be considered as a progressive application of technologies to meet business goals. The basic steps--digitize, organize, automate, and transform--are necessarily dependent on one another. For instance, data must first be digitized to be (digitally) organized. Likewise, it is impossible to implement automation without having a known, organized structuring of data. Automation requires regularity in the execution environment and structure in the underlying data. Transformation aligns and augments existing automation to accomplish specific business objectives. Because these steps are comprised of inescapable dependencies, organizations have encountered common problems and challenges. These are an inevitable result of emergent properties latent and initially unrecognized in implemented projects that were not identified and considered during planning phases.

In practical terms, most organizations follow a similar progression in their adoption of digital technology.

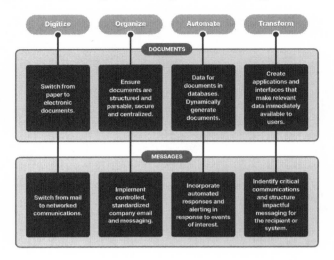

- Data is "digitized." Paper assets are converted into spreadsheets and documents.

- Data is extracted, transformed, and loaded (ETL) into databases in a manual/ad-hoc fashion.

- Data is made available via web applications and reporting systems, and isolated APIs.

- Data integration is systematized by implementing regular, scheduled, automated ETL processes.

- APIs are orchestrated to extend and regularize the availability of data.

These steps have an unfortunate side effect: they cause a company to organize itself around the systems built, rather than the customer or a business objective! This unintentional effect has been identified using the term affordance.[31] It is an

31 https://www.merriam-webster.com/dictionary/affordance

all-too-familiar outcome resulting from an overemphasis on technology in a vacuum. The progression, as listed, makes no mention of customer concerns. There is no explicit reference to business value.

Like the foundation of a house, these steps are essential. Work that follows is inextricably dependent on them. But a foundation alone does not enable daily living until the rest of the house is built. The house is then a home, fully functional, delivering personal value. Likewise, digital transformation builds upon foundational early efforts with an eye toward customer experience and specific business value.

From Data in Systems to Interfaces with Capabilities

In transformation within an organization, early automation efforts focus on centralizing and structuring data, typically in relatively isolated systems specific to a smaller group or department. This improves the ability of individuals to reliably obtain data for compartmentalized decision-making. Further work is required to make data across the organization available uniformly and consistently, enabling enterprise-wide, data-driven decision-making. Similarly, automated transactions between organizations are far more effective and efficient if they span business concerns. When systems across the organization are enabled to act in a coordinated manner, all parties have the same view of the data, eliminating confusion and entire classes of disagreements resulting from data anomalies, stale data, and other inconsistencies.

Without this later transformational effort, data is rarely available and leveraged across the organization. Since data management is essential and automation necessarily involves the creation of software systems, most organizations have matured to overcome a basic barrier to entry required of businesses operating at scale in the modern economy. Once this is in place, a company organizes staff and projects around the data and systems. An unfortunate side effect of concentrating on systems and underlying data structures is that it tends to shape conversations in a way that ignores the original intentions they were implemented to address. This makes the user experience a secondary concern and promotes "silos" of isolated, special purpose systems and databases that do not address business concerns in a coordinated manner. Digital transformation can remedy this situation by addressing the actual underlying business concerns, rather than slipping into cycles of software maintenance that do not positively impact outcomes.

The traditional idea of "integration" focuses on connecting systems, with the goal of sharing data between systems. This perspective is valuable and, at times, necessary, but it is better to reorient the focus of integration to the creation of clear, accessible, well-documented interfaces between capabilities.

Capabilities vs. Systems

Fundamentally, a capability is simply the ability to perform a function. It encompasses an action that is part of a business process. As such, it is implemented using systems but should not be thought of as specifically related to any given system. There is an unfortunate tendency to abandon the capability mindset once a specific tool or system is implemented. At that point, the focus shifts to the system even if it doesn't adequately represent the capability it was designed to address.

The divergence between capabilities and systems is evident in communication between business and technical staff. Business users are concerned with capabilities, but usually without a clear understanding of specific ties to available data, systems, or technology. Technical staff is acutely aware of systems and what they can do, but easily loses sight of the business goals when focused on technical considerations and system limitations. Conflicts that arise from this divergence often result in each group attempting to operate independently. The technical staff occupies itself with system upgrades, maintaining system stability, and handling support in a piecemeal manner. Business staff uses the systems, but creates kludgy workarounds and derivative data sources such as documents and spreadsheets to complete its work. This bifurcation needs to be avoided to derive the maximum value for the business. Digital transformation seeks to remedy the situation by requiring both parties to be actively involved and interact. Business users describe user activity and business needs, and technical staff provides implementation options to shape the business around those specific concerns.

An implemented software system includes a vast amount of embedded business knowledge. Rules about how the business operates, domain-specific calculations, and relationships between business entities are preserved in a system that ensures uniform processing for all users. But business users must ascertain changes in the business over time and understand how well the system is mapping to the current scenario. There is a tendency toward complacency that lends itself to blindly allowing a system to become an infallible source of truth and an unchangeable interface into how the business is conducted. Businesses must understand their current and desired capabilities. They must continuously evaluate how those capabilities map to existing and planned systems, and then work to maintain alignment between the two.

Interfaces vs. Connections

When a competent software developer is asked about the possibility of connecting any two digital systems, the developer will likely reply that it is possible and launch into a set of practical and theoretical considerations. Standard protocols might exist for connectivity. Translation layers may need to be written. Security must be considered. The frequency of data updates, scheduling of batch processes, and overall system performance will be discussed. What can be lost in this type of conversation is the fact that highly customized one-off connections between systems can be costly to support over time and are not easily generalizable if a third system that needs to connect in a similar way is introduced.

An interface is a general-purpose abstraction that allows connectivity with other systems. Properly designed, it is not limited to connectivity to only one other system. Any other system that must perform a similar data exchange can be configured to use the interface. Consistent implementation of interfaces is cheaper and easier to support in a standardized way over time. API orchestration allows managing data transactions between various services where requests and responses need to be split, merged, or routed.

A metric for measuring the success of systems connectivity is how quickly a new system can be added. The idea of clean interfaces over digital capabilities is not a focus on the systems themselves. Instead, the focus of any work in the organization is to promote business agility to obtain specific business results, regardless of the systems involved.

Interfaces can grow and mature over time. Various versions of APIs serving as interfaces can be implemented that address changing business needs and new data formats. In addition, interfaces can be simplified over time, requiring corresponding flexibility in the supporting implementation. This pattern can be beneficial in that it allows a certain amount of leniency when dealing with external systems. The tradeoff is that the associated service needs to include conditional logic designed to accommodate all input variations.

The primacy of interfaces has been expressed in various ways in recent years. For example, Jeff Bezos's move to mandate the availability of usable interfaces to all systems was pivotal and revolutionized Amazon's business.[32] The push for "service-oriented architectures" in previous years was a technical attempt to shift enterprises in this direction. Digital transformation involves higher- level business concepts that can benefit from similar technical design concerns.

Orbweaver Perspective: Project Execution

In working with electronic companies, we created a unified platform that allows businesses to take advantage of interfaces that expose business capabilities within their organization and when interacting with customers and partners. A specific example is DataHub middleware. DataHub is a data integration tool that connects Orbweaver's clients to their customers, suppliers, and data providers. Regardless of the data type or structure, DataHub acts as a translator, connecting systems and companies seamlessly to each other. It enables digital connections to any of a business's customers, suppliers, or internal systems.1

---

1   https://www.orbweaver.com/products/datahub/

Buy vs. Build

There are various options available for unifying and managing an API layer to create interfaces between business capabilities. These include custom solutions, API management platforms, andsector-specific platforms. Like all technical solutions, there are trade-offs for each and there is no "one-size-fits-all" way to resolve problems.

The first option is for organizations to build custom solutions. This work requires software architecture analysis to mandate the design and deployment patterns used across all business units. Management of this type of project involves a full, end-to-end software development life cycle and quality assurance

---

32 https://gist.github.com/chitchcock/1281611

testing in dedicated test environments. This approach is clearly resource-intensive and requires deep expertise into software development practices that is not available in many organizations. When available, this is the most highly customizable solution.

Another option is use of an API management platform. Apigee[33] and MuleSoft[34] are two well-known options. Both vendors offer cloud-based and on-premise solutions. These platforms are supported by large companies and geared toward a generic audience. The systems are not specific to the electronics industry or any other type of business. Engagements frequently include the involvement of special purpose software development consultants that stand up systems and hand them off to company systems administrators to maintain. This type of solution provides a relatively stable, mature platform without requiring the same degree of technical involvement required by a customized solution.

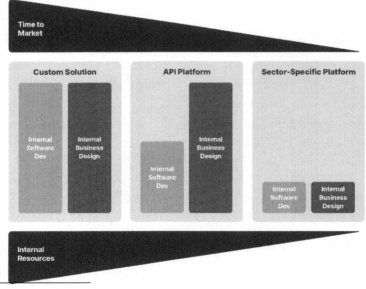

33 https://cloud.google.com/apigee/
34 https://www.mulesoft.com/

You can think of the options available as the inverse of a "sell or process further" decision. It's a "buy or do more processing yourself" decision. A customized solution requires little up-front payment to external entities but an immense amount of technical work that must be done over time. An API platform reduces the work involved. A dedicated solution geared specifically to your business incurs the lowest internal effort and expense.

Partner Services vs. Consultancies

The partner vs. build discussion omits consideration of general-purpose consulting firms (like Accenture, IBM, or Deloitte). Consultants can be valuable contributors to specific, well-defined products, but are problematic for broader digital transformation efforts. On the other hand, partnerships create a strong alignment of incentives between organizations entering into a digital transformation project with a broader, more dynamic project scope.

These assertions are based on the time horizon typical to each type of entity.

- Consultancies avoid consequences. Consultancies are typically contracted to create a system, deploy it, and deliver it within a relatively short period of time to internal operational support. Partners provide initial integration as well as ongoing support. Partners live with the consequences of their actions and therefore have greater motivation to see the project successfully implemented.

- Consultants limit long-term support. Consultancy agreements typically imply that the product they create can later be easily supported internally. It is rarely possible to obtain ongoing high-level support. Consultants who are skilled at software development in specific technologies develop systems that are handed off to internal staff. Internal staff is often not capable of supporting basic operational concerns. Partnerships involve long-term, dedicated support as part of an offering.

• Consultants often deploy immature products. Consultants often work on a project but don't stay to ensure full production operational capabilities. Their work is often approved in the context of small scale, individual demos. Consultants don't provide ongoing support for a multi-user system. As a result, they may miss problems that only manifest when systems experience production load. Areas affected include multiuser transactional concerns such as blocking, performance at scale, monitoring and alert tooling, ongoing software updates, and database updates supported via database migrations.

Example: Part Pricing

The pricing of electronic parts is a very complex activity. The responsibility and ownership of assigning part prices involves multiple teams. Agreements and contracts between suppliers and buyers govern customer-specific pricing arrangements. Business process must consistently designate and apply rules to calculate, approve, and present part prices. Additional complexities include pricing updates, special promotions, and volume discounts. These complexities can result in a fragmented, inconsistent experience for buyers and inefficient assignment of prices by suppliers.

As illustrated below, an organization consists of multiple teams that participate in pricing activity. Team members might actively assign prices, calculate profit margins, incorporate comparisons with competing products, specify contracts with purchasers, address questions regarding regulatory standards for product categories, or track and maintain inventory. All of these considerations might interest an end user, but the experience of obtaining related information and making a purchase can be fragmented, requiring the reconciliation of resources obtained via phone calls, paper catalogs, and online resources.

It is not uncommon for each department involved to utilize a separate and distinct data store and software system. A certain amount of integration is likely available, but it is common for each department to effectively organize around a given system as its "source of truth." The integration available is often initially created as "one-off" processes. Examples might be an API for the parts catalog system used by the corporate sales portal, or a CSV extract from the corporate sales portal that is imported into the ERP system daily.

A comprehensive digital transformation effort recognizes these resources and their value but approaches the problem from the perspective of an end user—in this case, the buyer interested in researching and purchasing parts.

A buyer isn't interested in the specific systems involved or which teams are responsible for their maintenance. A user might be interested in searching for a product and wants to immediately know not only the customer-specific price of the part, but also its regulatory classification for inclusion in a government contract and how many parts are currently in inventory. Such a request spans marketing, price management, sales, legal, and inventory teams.

The API orchestration / ETL process layer can start as a simple set of standards rather than an integrated platform, and be expanded over time, but this requires a great deal of organizational effort since no single department is specifically interested in this broader concern. This is why many organizations standardize on a platform early on, and integrate individual departments as the demands that they integrate and participate in grow.

Technology Terms

API orchestration and ETL processes have grown up around a set of technologies that describe formats used to represent data and the methods used to transfer the data. We close this chapter with a description of some of the most common technologies you are likely to encounter when discussing data transfer required for digital transformation.

Note that the descriptions are technology agnostic. There are numerous relational databases in use including open-source offerings like MySQL, MariaDB, PostgreSQL as well as commercial implementations like Oracle and Microsoft SQL Server. There are NoSQL databases including MongoDB and Cassandra. Data stored in these systems or elsewhere can be served in APIs built using various programming languages including Java, .NET, Ruby, Python, and others. ETL tools typically leverage database drivers implemented for each language along with SQL. The terms below are not tied to these or any other technologies. They are abstractions that can be implemented using the technologies listed earlier, as well as others.

Time/Processing Designations

Realtime or synchronous solutions provide nearly immediate transfers of small amounts of data in response to a request.

Batch processing is the asynchronous exchange of large amounts of data, often in response to a file system event or scheduled job trigger.

Batch Processing

Extract-transform-load pipelines (ETL) are used to process files of data periodically. Structured query language (SQL) queries are used to extract data from relational databases. A subset of SQL called DML (data manipulation language) is used to insert, update, or delete data in relational databases.

Data Transfer Protocols

TCP/IP is a set of communication protocols used on the Internet and similar computer networks. The foundational protocols are Transmission Control Protocol (TCP) and Internet Protocol (IP). Two application-level protocols are of particular interest for supporting APIs and ETL within an organization:

Hypertext Transfer Protocol (HTTP) is a protocol for transmitting documents and is the foundation of the World Wide Web. The content type—or media type (MIME type)—specifies the format of the body of the content. Web browsers or other systems act as clients and make requests to servers that respond based on the nature of the request. The request consists of a request method—GET and POST being the most popular—and a reference to the resource of interest using uniform resource locators (URLs). The response includes the requested resource as well as a response code. Various headers included in the request and response can include further information about how to process a request or response. Secure communication can be obtained using HTTPS where requests and responses are encrypted using transport layer security (TLS).

File Transfer Protocol (FTP) is specifically used to transmit files. Like HTTP, it supports secure transmissions via extensions that leverage encryption as part of the protocol.

Data Formats

Hypertext Markup Language (HTML) is the standard markup language for documents served over HTTP to be displayed in a web browser. It consists of a set of predefined tags specifying the format and appearance of a web page. It is used in conjunction with technologies like Cascading Style Sheets (CSS) and JavaScript to augment the appearance and behavior of modern websites.

Extensible Markup Language (XML) is similar to HTML but does not specify predefined tags. Rather than being used with display purposes in mind (like HTML), it is used to describe data in a structured manner. A host of XML-related technologies were developed to provide additional validation, querying, and transformation of XML documents.

JavaScript Object Notation (JSON) is a subset of JavaScript used as a data-interchange format. A JSON document representing the same information as a corresponding XML document is smaller and often easier for humans to read.

API Protocols

The data formats and data transfer protocols detailed above are built upon to create API protocols that follow a set of relatively standard patterns. In general, XML or JSON over HTTP can be used in various ways to create an API.

Representational State Transfer (REST) is a software architectural style. It is commonly implemented in practice as XML or JSON over HTTP. HTTP methods are used to create (POST), read (GET), update (PATCH or PUT), and destroy (DELETE) resources. Systems built in this manner consider endpoint resources as nouns modeling a domain that is acted upon. In its original form, REST described an efficient way of using HTTP. As such, many of the details of HTTP are evident in implementations when compared with legacy protocols.

Remote Procedure Call (RPC) models a system's endpoints as representing verbs – actions to be taken to modify the system's state. Like REST, it is typically implemented over HTTP. Some APIs use a combination of REST and RPC to define APIs.

Other protocols and formats extend the basic ones listed above in various ways. For instance, Google Remote Procedure Call (gRPC) is an RPC system developed in 2015. Rather than JSON, the most commonly used IDL (interface definition language) for gRPC is a binary interchange format called protocol buffers, or Protobuf, an extensible mechanism for serializing structured data.

Legacy Protocols

Recently developed API protocols are much simpler and, ironically, more open-ended than legacy protocols. Legacy protocols were designed to run over HTTP as well as alternatives like simple mail transfer protocol (SMTP).

Electronic data interchange (EDI) involves document exchanges of information that was traditionally communicated on paper, including purchase orders, invoices, and other standard business documents. It has been around in various forms since the 1970s. EDI uses connections between two EDI systems, whereas an API uses a web-based protocol that allows different systems to communicate with each other. It was further described in various standards such as the Electronic Data Interchange for Administration, Commerce, and Transport (EDIFACT) and X12. This legacy approach involves asynchronous batch exchange of large amounts of data, whereas APIs typically are synchronous, real-time transfers of smaller amounts of data. EDI can use web-based protocols like HTTP or FTP as well as higher level protocols built on these, such as AS2 and AS3.

Simple object access protocol (SOAP) is a messaging protocol specification for exchanging structured XML documents generally over HTTP. Because SOAP can be implemented using different underlying protocols (not just HTTP), it reimplemented functionality found in HTTP like error reporting, caching, and addressing of requests.

Security Concerns

Software developers often use frameworks that provide security functionality. These tend to map to a few basic underlying areas of security. Security is a complex and sensitive topic, but unavoidable in most real-world projects. The areas listed are representative of areas that will be discussed in most API/web application integration projects, but they are by no means an exhaustive list:

- Web applications historically supported internally maintained authentication using a username and password via basic authentication. Form-based authentication largely superseded basic authentication, as it could be customized by developers to a greater extent than is available for basic authentication. There is also one lesser-used method known as digest authentication, an application of MD5 cryptographic hashing with the usage of nonce values.

• Web applications have shifted toward using externally managed identity solutions. OAuth 2.0 is a set of specifications defining the delegation of authentication and authorization to external providers. There are many ways that OAuth is configured and used today.[35] Open ID Connect is an identity layer built on top of OAuth 2.0.[36]

• Encryption is the process of cryptographically encoding information. Various encryption strategies are available that use various algorithms with different properties. Public-key encryption specifies a public key to be published for general use and to encrypt messages, as well as a private decryption key for restricted usage by a single user that enables messages to be read. The encryption of data to obtain security can be applied when data is stored (security at rest) or when it is in the process of being transferred between systems (security in transit). Encryption at rest and encryption in transit are common designations but do not capture additional points where data encryption might apply (encrypting data in memory during processing or in messages that appear in log files).

---

35 https://fusionauth.io/learn/expert-advice/oauth/modern-guide-to-oauth/

36 https://openid.net/connect/

This area has been called encryption at work[37] and has found its way into some web application frameworks.[38] The descriptions above are not comprehensive but provide the basic groundwork to discuss options for digital transformation involving web APIs and ETL.

---

37 https://www.hey.com/security/#:~:text=At%2Dwork%20encryption%20means%20that,encrypted%20with%20a%20master%20key

38 https://rubyonrails.org/2021/12/6/
Rails-7-0-rc-1-released#at-work-encryption-with-active-record

8

Data and Digital Transformation

Much of this book has addressed digital transformation from a comprehensive, outward-facing perspective. Rather than looking at isolated systems, its focus has been on people doing business a certain way, the processes they use, and their overall organizational goals. This chapter is devoted to data, an internal, specific concern.

Data is the raw material being managed and updated in response to business activities. This shift in emphasis from broad organizational concerns to the data is intended to highlight data assets at our disposal and the effort, energy, and attention required to manage in the context of specific projects.

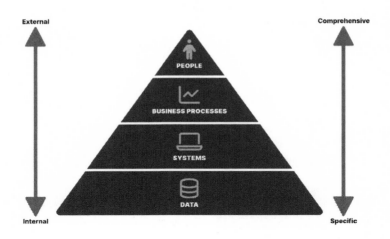

This shift in emphasis is needed to understand the whole perspective provided by digital transformation. Digital transformation projects meet in the middle of the triangle shown. Digital assets and systems are organized and revised to align with dynamic business processes and requirements of individual people conducting business. It's a mistake to ignore the people and processes in a business. Designing a sweeping digital architecture is also problematic if the underlying data sources and systems are not identified and understood.

The digital world ultimately can be decomposed into zeroes and ones, built layer upon layer to produce a model that, in some sense, emulates or represents the real world. The nuances and complexities of the real world can never be fully captured in this medium, so data stored digitally is ultimately a limited abstraction of real-world entities. As a result, there is an "impedance mismatch" that must be overcome at various locations in the enterprise. This incongruity can cause problems when users interact with applications or when relationships and exchanges are reduced to representations processed by computerized workflows. In each case, real-world entities are stored incompletely, but hopefully accurately, in digital form. Digital transformation recognizes this incongruity and seeks to align digital resources better to match the current real-world situation and highlight items of interest. We start by considering the available data and how it is being managed.

Data Sources

Organizations store data digitally, but not in the most organized, efficient, and seamless way. An enormous amount of valuable data is trapped in spreadsheets on an individual's workstation. A first step in mitigating this problem is to add shared directories and centralized document stores. But identifying which spreadsheet is canonical is challenging. Data can be imported into databases but is frequently siloed in systems, preventing all but the most technical users who have sufficient application privileges and adequate business knowledge from effectively joining data across systems. Regarding the data itself, digital transformation efforts seek to better organize and link disparate data sources.

Before attempting to transform a company, it is important to catalog what data is available and where it is located. This provides a better understanding of when new systems need to be built and what access points should be created. It might also reveal redundant systems that can be combined, or even highlight those that would be better managed if separated into separate systems. This is a daunting task that involves consistency and organizational skills to capture information relevant to a particular project. Ideally, cataloging data is an ongoing activity assigned to, and performed by, a specific team member.

Much of the subsequent discussion assumes data stored in relational databases. Non-relational databases generally support analogous functionality, including query languages, connection protocols, and access management. Despite their ubiquity, spreadsheets are not a particularly manageable source for canonical data that is fundamental to an organization's primary business functions. Data in spreadsheets is inherently difficult to manage, validate, audit, and control. So in most cases, it is important to commit widely used, business-critical data to relational databases to derive further benefit.

Data Flow

After gaining clarity on the available data sources, it's important to understand where data comes from and how it is updated. The flow of data must be traced from its point of origin. As it moves through the organization and is transformed over time, points that are stale, overwritten, or underutilized can be identified. Validation points throughout the process should be standardized to ensure that consistent, normalized versions of data are available for consumption. New and updated data will be introduced to the system through applications, APIs, and data loading processes. While the flow of data is remarkably complex and challenging to quantify objectively, quantification is a prerequisite for measurable improvement. Understanding and controlling data flow—at least in the most significant cases—is essential to improving data usage.

Data Access

A related concern to the flow of data is data access. This includes networking (firewall configuration and port availability), database connectivity using protocols like ODBC or JDBC, authentication and authorization of database users, and related software drivers installed on machines requiring data access. The flow of data out of, and into, databases occurs in the form of queries (or DML statements), data imports/extracts, API, and web application activity. Each of these requires user and access management that affects the security and availability of data for use across business silos.

Data Retrieval

Data analysts and data scientists within your organization leverage tools utilizing query languages, notably SQL, to extract and transform tabular data using a relatively small number of basic operations. Several are practical implementations of relational algebra[39], which is based on a formal system of well-founded semantics. Practically speaking, many of these operations have implementations in spreadsheet software. These include projections (limiting columns in view) and filtering (limiting which rows are in view by defining criteria for inclusion or exclusion). In addition, relational databases provide options to combine and aggregate datasets for which there is no specific analog in spreadsheet software (although Microsoft Excel does provide the VLOOKUP function and/or tools like Power Query[40]). Finally sorting tabular data, which is not a formal property of sets, is also available in standard query languages.

Operation	SQL Keyword
Limit Columns	SELECT
Limit Rows	WHERE, HAVING
Combine tables	JOIN (including inner and various outer joins), UNION (and other set operations)
Aggregate	GROUP BY with analytical functions in the SELECT clause
Sorting	ORDER BY

SQL is a declarative language. It specifies *what* data is required rather than *how* to retrieve it. Unfortunately, software developers tend to be trained in procedural languages that specify nitty-gritty details about how to change a data structure. This

---

39 https://en.wikipedia.org/wiki/Relational_algebra

40 https://docs.microsoft.com/en-us/power-query/power-query-what-is-power-query

provides a great deal of control, but frankly is limiting in many situations. Having a working knowledge of what is possible with SQL will help facilitate discussions that require a somewhat formal and specific description of the data in use.

Data Import / Update

Several standard practices implemented across databases can address typical business concerns that tend to arise after a system is built. These include database auditing–ensuring that who changed what and when is tracked and reported. Another is enforcing standards related to names of columns, particularly primary and foreign keys. Surrogate keys are often preferable to natural primary keys to ensure that changing business requirements don't destroy a data model and disrupt corresponding relationships with other tables. Using sequential numeric IDs for primary keys is often a useful practice. However, there are cases where data is expected to be exported/imported between related databases, and UUIDs should be used to avoid conflicts. These functions are easy to build into a system early on, but if they are not, there is often no way to backport missing prior data.

Data Architecture

The above topics are typically beyond a business user's scope, more familiar to data analysts, data scientists, and database administrators. There is value to having a dedicated data architect to own data concerns, establish standards that span systems, and encourage consistency throughout the organization.

The conversation on data retrieval touched upon the discipline of data modeling. Data modeling tends to be specific to a system or database. The more comprehensive view of data architecture spans multiple systems and seeks data integration and availability across the enterprise. As such, it is aligned with digital transformation in its tendency to reduce silos and establish open, consistent data availability across the organization. Those performing the architecture role must model systems, both individually and collectively. They author and establish organizational data policies, rules, and standards to define how data is collected, stored, and used.

Due to the ad-hoc, emergent manner in which data is managed, it is unsurprising that many organizations do not have a dedicated data architect. In any case, participating systems, their capabilities, and the data they house must be understood for management and utilization. For this reason, it is often necessary to meet with a number of different system owners and maintainers to construct a sufficient data architecture representation in the furthering of digital transformation initiatives.

Principles

There are a number of principles or general standards that data architects are guided by, regardless of specific organizational goals. Data architects are responsible for ensuring data is classified, useful, understandable, and available, regardless of the specifics of the company or business domain. Responsibilities that fall upon official and de facto data architects include the following:

Standardize Data Vocabulary

Common vocabularies promote common understanding across the organization. The electronic industry and individual companies use a good deal of jargon that can be a useful shorthand when commonly understood, but is otherwise a source of confusion. In addition, specific analytics and KPI definitions involve a degree of precision not clearly captured in informal conversations. The standard data vocabulary should be documented with training provided to encourage accurate communication and subsequent decision-making.

Monitor Data Quality

Data quality will be discussed in greater detail below. Data architects must certainly identify data duplication across the organization, establish canonical representations of duplicated data, and both measure and improve the accuracy of data and its overall relevance for business decisions. This effort also relates to the flow of data--tracking transformation and changes--as it moves through the organization.

Promote Data Availability

Data is ideally readily available and not unnecessarily hidden from those who would benefit from its use. Departmental data silos often must be eliminated, providing an extensive general means of accessing data outside of the department where it originated. This concern must be balanced with security and privacy concerns that limit data to be available only to authorized parties when the data is actually needed. But there are many cases where limits on data access are incidental to system design or historic processes, thus failing to address any actual security or privacy concerns.

Organizational Management

People (data architects and professionals serving in this role) enact changes and policies related to a business's use of data. People implement and maintain the platforms used to store the data. The organizational concerns required to set the goals that will guide specific data-related projects fall under a number of common headings.

Data Strategy

The general intention of a data strategy is to promote a data-driven culture where decisions are made based on objective, quantifiable criteria. The strategy seeks to balance competing areas like availability vs. security, quality validation vs. other quality concerns, backup, recovery and availability within budgetary constraints, and data maintenance locations (on premise, in cloud storage, etc.). The strategy provides the foundational vision for defining governance, quality, and operational concerns. It ensures effective and efficient use of data to enable the organization to achieve its business goals.

Data Governance

Data governance seeks to describe roles, standards, and metrics based on the data strategy. These ensure that the data is usable, available, and only accessible to those authorized to view or change it. Data governance includes policies related to process changes to data and databases. It provides the underlying requirements for improving and managing data quality through data operations.

Data Quality

A variety of standard data quality measures can be used to describe data quality quantitatively.

Completeness indicates whether the data is sufficient to be applied to a given use. Missing data and null values are a source of a great deal of confusion for reporting and processing. Null values and missing data can represent many things – data that is missing, data that is unavailable, data that is forthcoming, etc. Processing incomplete data can be very complex. In some cases, values are substituted from missing data, while in others all records missing any data are thrown out. Even when accurate results can be obtained, the existence of missing data remains a source of confusion due to the extra processing required.

Accuracy describes the degree to which data represents the real-world referent.

Consistency signifies whether the same data stored in different places matches. When there is any drift, it is important to clearly understand the data flow and designate the canonical value that applies at a given time in a given context. A related concern is **timeliness,** which ensures information is available when it is expected and needed (and any divergence is readily understood).

Validity assesses whether data is within understood bounds or ranges appropriate to the domain. Data type, size, and format apply at a minimum. Certain values might be designated "out of bounds" or impossible values that cannot exist in the real world. Other values might be considered unique.

Uniqueness ensures no duplication or overlaps exist in data, based on criteria for designating it "one of a kind."

Integrity indicates the degree that data can be traced/linked across datasets (including datasets across systems).

Many other concerns might be considered aspects of data quality, but drift into other areas.

- Data should ideally be relevant (or eliminated if it is not).

- A value should be interpretable, that is, in a form that the target audience can utilize for the intended purpose.

- Data should be worth more than the cost to store it, so cost effectiveness measures might also apply.

- Applications that require data from multiple data sources might value a variety of data sources.

- Based on data governance policies and the overall data strategy, an appropriate set of metrics can be identified and used to provide a baseline data quality that can be periodically updated and monitored over time.

Data Operations

Data operations involves people, processes, and systems that enable an organization to achieve data governance and quality goals. In general, proper data operations promote consistent data quality, secure access to data, and relevant automation to avoid manual errors and inconsistencies. Data operations accomplishes this through management of the various databases and data storage systems, their access, and the flow of data to and from the systems.

Implicit Management via Affordances

There are corollaries relevant to data operations related to a problem cited in Chapter 7. The problem discussed involves people organizing their work around system limitations and boundaries, rather than customer or business objectives. This is because systems exist in a context and are designed (consciously or unconsciously) to provide *affordances*. An affordance is not a "property" of an object or system (like a UI screen or web API endpoint). An affordance is defined in the relation between the user and the object. It describes the possible interactions between the user and the object.

Affordances can result in ill effects when not considered, but, once recognized, they can be used to design better systems.

One positive affordance related to data operations is that *adequately designed systems encourage people to adjust the way they work to be better aligned with organizational goals.* A subtle but powerful managerial influence can thus be exercised as a part of digital transformation. This is accomplished by designing systems that enforce workflows and interactions among participating actors. The beneficial result can be better quality data, more consistent data and results, and consolidation of disparate processing patterns, among others.

The value of recognizing affordances is how they can direct people's behavior without requiring training, persuasion, or direct management. It can be challenging to convince people to adopt new behaviors or revise familiar processes. However, it is possible to create systems with constraints that implicitly direct people to do "the right thing" and discourage "the wrong thing." By understanding your users and their goals, you can also create systems that provide better information to the user and a better overall experience that provides positive feedback to employees who are more satisfied with the work they can accomplish.

People tend to gravitate toward the path of least resistance when seeking to complete their work. They are not always completely aware of the assumptions built into their work or the broader context of its impact. The specific goal of an individual contributor can be aligned via proper system design to enable them the ability and satisfaction to do good work while also promoting organizational goals and maintaining related standards. This type of system design applies to many areas but is extremely important regarding data operations.

A simple example common in the sphere of data operations is the design of user interfaces related to data validation. Allowing free-form text entry tends to result in a large amount of poor quality data that needs to be manually reviewed and normalized to be useful. However, if a known requirement is that a given data value is required and must have a valid value, a UI that requires that the user select a valid value from a list, rather than entering it by hand, is preferable. The user does not need to deal with any uncertainty about what value should be entered, and the organization is not faced with a data quality problem to resolve later.

Implicit management via system design can also span systems. For example, all new additions to a parts catalog can be added using a single web service that centralizes validation and normalization of data values and addresses other concerns. All systems requiring catalog data would call the single web service that manages the catalog data. Any alternative methods to adding parts would be disallowed as part of the implementation. The consistency of a single system is far easier to support and troubleshoot for the organization. And if there is no alternative mechanism for updating the catalog (and the API is performant, responsive, and otherwise works as expected), users have a better experience completing their work.

Data Storage

Data storage is a wide-ranging but unavoidable topic. A few broad concepts are worth considering when evaluating a new data storage system.

Data Usage Patterns

Regardless of organization, certain tensions in data usage patterns are inevitable. It is necessary to have easy-to-implement, prefabricated global historical reporting available for general consumption across the business. It is also advantageous to allow ad hoc data analysis and exploratory efforts to power users and technical staff. Properly implemented reports

Orbweaver Perspective: Project Execution

CTO Tony Powell notes the challenge faced with the deluge of data: "Businesses are required to store, analyze, and maintain huge amounts of data using highly specialized technologies and techniques. We have found many opportunities where it is simply easier and more cost efficient for a business to use the Orbweaver platform and the collective experience encapsulated in it rather than hiring teams of professionals and building their own systems."

provide a sound foundation for communication across various departments in an organization. Ad hoc exploratory analysis is inevitably required due to swift changes in market conditions or the business environment that cannot be quickly reflected in standard reports.

Reports reflect the need for structure and control in data usage. Ad hoc exploratory analysis reflects the need for flexibility. This tension is evident in most financial organizations where an ERP provides structured data and pre-canned reports, but much of the organization uses spreadsheets to compensate for the ERP's lack of flexibility. Digital transformation efforts can mitigate this tension in cases where an application (or partner platform) uses data from established systems, but makes it available to users in a far more focused, accessible manner.

Storing Data Once vs. Many Times

There are valid reasons for storing data once in a single location versus the opposing principle of storing data in multiple locations. When data is stored in only one place, there is no question about which version is valid, or about which system provides the best access. There is even a process in database design known as normalization specifically targeted at eliminating duplicate storage of data in a given database. However, the use of caches to improve performance is a well-accepted standard practice that requires the duplication of data. In some cases, it is possible to have a well-accepted central data storage location as well as well-understood caches at various places. This is an acceptable compromise in that it provides the benefits of caching without sacrificing the identity of the canonical data source. Such a clear compromise is not always possible, but it is important to keep the challenges in mind in planning related to data storage.

Application vs. Integration Database

Martin Fowler distinguishes two styles of databases:[41]

- An application database is a backing store for a single application. It is easier to modify and can have a more concrete schema since it is not attempting to serve a broader, more general audience.

- An integration database is a database that acts as the data store for multiple applications. Its schema tends to be more general, more complex, or both.

This distinction is clear at project inception, but often becomes muddied over time. In practice, most successful databases in the enterprise become integration databases as additional ETL processes and services are bolted on over time.

Logical Model vs. Physical Data Storage

The logical model references the form and location in which data appears to an end user or client program. This includes relationships between various entities, attributes associated with entities, and their data types. Physical data storage references the files stored on actual hardware and disk locations where data is persisted. The independence between physical deployment and logical models is evident when comparing

41 https://www.martinfowler.com/bliki/DatabaseStyles.html

relational databases. For instance, an SQLite database is stored in a single file[42], while MySQL provides an option to store data associated with each table in a single file.[43] Each of these examples maintains a fairly clear mapping between the logical structures and physical files. Distributed database systems (like Oracle RAC), which utilize files stored on multiple servers, maintain a far less clear mapping between the two.

The logical model is squarely in view in discussions with developers writing software that queries and modifies data in the database. Physical storage is especially relevant to system administration staff and database administrators. Physical storage tends to be the focus when discussing the costs of cloud deployments, questions about replication, backup/recovery processes, and overall availability considerations.

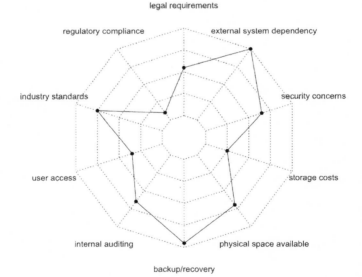

42 https://www.sqlite.org/onefile.html#:~:text=Single%2Dfile%20 Cross%2Dplatform%20Database,machine%20with%20a%20 different%20architecture

43 https://dev.mysql.com/doc/refman/5.6/en/innodb-file-per-table-ta-blespaces.html

A theme in digital transformation success is cross-functional participation. Data storage policy is an area that highlights this need. System operators are highly focused on user access. Database administrators are likely sensitive to physical space requirements, storage costs, and backup recovery processes. But technical personnel often have little insight into internal auditing standards, industry standards, and legal compliance. Breaking down silos necessarily adds complexity to global enforcement of storage policies, but the risks involved are too expensive to sidestep conversations on this topic when implementing a project.

Structured vs. Unstructured Data

Structured data is organized into specific entities, attributes, and types and is stored in a predefined logical format. Unstructured data is a conglomeration of many varied types of data that are stored without clearly defined formats. Data doesn't always fall into neat categories; the term "semi-structured data" captures cases that lie somewhere in between these two extremes. It is important to understand that naive classifications (e.g. text documents are unstructured, spreadsheets are semi-structured, relational databases are structured) are not always useful, and there is a significant tradeoff on data ingesting and reporting when dealing with different types of data.

There is a continuum between structured and unstructured data. A relational database is designed to support structured data storage but can be used to store data in an unstructured format. For example, a binary object representing a picture of a hand-scrawled note is certainly an example of unstructured data but can easily be stored as a binary large object (BLOB) in a relational database. A particularly challenging example is found in arbitrary PDF files. These can be created in a highly structured manner (typically generated via automation) but can be semi-structured (when manually created by a person) or even completely unstructured (a PDF that has content consisting of a scanned image).

Structured data typically requires more processing, transformation, and validation when it is stored, while unstructured data takes minimal effort. The converse is true when retrieving and correlating data: structured data lends itself to straightforward summarization and reporting, while unstructured data often requires a large amount of additional processing, transformation, and validation on the way out of the system. Reporting can be adjusted late in a project when using structured data in relational databases. It cannot be easily changed when unstructured data is involved, especially if it is in certain NoSQL databases where data indexes and access patterns must be understood and defined up front.

Small vs. "Big Data"

The term "big data" has been discussed a great deal in recent years and generally does not have a well- understood meaning in every context. People are notoriously bad at conceptualizing large numbers and the improvements in processing power and storage over the course of time. There are ongoing discussions[44] between professionals that attempt to definitively identify what qualifies as big data. However, there is undeniably a set of techniques and technologies originating from companies (like Google) dealing with some of the largest datasets humanity has ever assembled.

Big data is typically applied to three areas: volume, velocity, and variety.

Volume

Volume means the amount of data stored. Cheap disks and cloud computing options now allow large amounts of data

---

44 https://datascience.stackexchange.com/questions/19/
how-big-is-big-data

to be stored. Following Google's lead, many organizations adopted distributed file systems frameworks (Hadoop) and certain NoSQL databases (Apache HBase). A major selling point of large amounts of relatively unstructured storage was that ETL processes could be effectively eliminated, and all data could be easily accessible in a corporate data lake.

The technology ecosystem (rather than the amount of data) is actually the defining characteristic of "big data" in many situations. As a rule of thumb, the volume of data can be classified by where it can be processed. Relatively "small" datasets can be viewed and manipulated in a spreadsheet on an individual's workstation. "Medium" data can be handled in monolithic (server-hosted) databases. "Big" data tends to be processed using Hadoop or other distributed databases.

A more nuanced discussion[45] of "big data" by Hadley Wickham points out two transition points for classifying data:

- From in memory to disk (this takes into account larger amounts of memory now available to computer workstations).

- From one computer to many computers.

Wickham also references three main classes of data problems:

- Big data problems that are actually small data problems (once your filter or summarize correctly).

- Big data problems that are several small data problems.

- True big data models requiring all available data in its complete and most detailed form. Certain machine learning problems fall definitively into this category.

---

45 https://dataconomy.com/2015/08/three-main-big-data-problems/

The possibility of saving a great deal of money and time through a detailed problem analysis is worth considering before investing heavily in a dedicated, internal big data platform.

Velocity

Velocity relates to how fast data is moving (e.g. how quickly it must be ingested or transferred between systems). Historically, reporting was done in long-running batch processes using data that was a bit "old" (from a previous day, week, or month). Big data velocity strives to provide real-time or nearly real-time access to information using highly parallel distributed processing like MapReduce, which also originated at Google.

Variety

Variety in big data refers to large amounts of incompatible, unstructured data objects being stored together. For instance, a mixture of human-created documents, machine-generated documents, images, sound files, videos, and other media might be included in a cloud storage system. Processing data that varies so greatly involves unique challenges, as there is no clear metadata reference that succinctly expresses what data is embedded in objects and is available during processing.

Current Point-in-Time Data vs. Historical

Many standard data modeling techniques represent the state of a system as the current "point in time." That is, the data stored is understood to indicate what is true at the moment. An alternative way of modeling data involves keeping track of all changes over time. This type of historical tracking of data provides an ongoing audit of data that can be used to determine "who changed what when." Understanding this distinction is important during system design, as there is no easy way to backfill historical changes if the data is not stored up front.

Certain databases (MariaDB using SYSTEM VERSION[46], Oracle via Flashback[47]) support tracking of data changes with built-in features. There are also other types of auditing available that track what queries are executed, not what changes are made. But depending on the specific requirements related to historical data involved, data retention policies, and operational procedures, database features might be insufficient to track the data as needed. Application-level processes can be used in such cases rather than relying on database-specific features.

Application-level auditing can be built using systems of triggers and tables which mirror current time application tables. A related application-level change can be implemented in systems where all historical changes need to be tracked. In such systems, true destruction of data must be eliminated. This can be done by implementing so called "soft-deletes" where a flag is added to each record that can be updated to indicate a record has been deleted. Like all application code, it must be maintained and supported over time by staff.

Storage Technologies

Data storage is a complex topic that has changed significantly with the advent of cloud-based services and options. In general, data storage is designed to support either structured or unstructured data.

---

46 https://mariadb.com/kb/en/system-versioned-tables/

47 https://docs.oracle.com/en/database/
oracle/oracle-database/21/adfns/flashback.
html#GUID-CAC23AAE-AD5A-47FA-B446-B4DE00B2B876

Unstructured

A traditional file server is simply a computer attached to a network that provides a location for shared disk access. Certain file systems include additional features, such as historical versioning as objects change (much like the git version control system used by software developers). File servers have given way to object stores that manage data as objects, rather than maintaining a hierarchy of files. Amazon S3 and Google Cloud Storage are cloud-based object stores, whereas Ceph and MinIO are open-source solutions. Each object store has slightly different features and interfaces, but there are similarities (MinIO is S3 compatible, for example).

Structured

Relational databases store data structured as tables containing rows (records) that have a defined structure. Each row contains columns specified as part of the table definition. Additional database objects assist search speed (indexes) or extend the relational model to include procedural processing (stored procedures, triggers, functions). Databases support transactional processing, which alleviates a number of data anomalies that can occur when data can be accessed and changed by multiple parties.

NoSQL databases provide an alternative to relational databases. These include a range of storage mechanisms, including columnar, key-value, graph, document, or object. Most NoSQL databases were designed to address a perceived weakness in available relational technology. They might provide better performance (on insert or retrieval), easier replication across systems, or support for data structures that are difficult to represent in a relational model. Most also sacrifice an aspect of the relational model to obtain their goals--a caveat often missed when preoccupied with the benefits a new system offers.

One special type of data store that provides remarkably fast query response times is a service that runs on a search engine library like Apache Lucene. Both Apache Solr and Elasticsearch are built using this specially designed index. Due to their effectiveness in returning initial results quickly, these services sometimes become de facto databases. Despite their usefulness, these products are best used strictly for indexing and search applications. Data is better managed outside of these indexes, allowing the indexes to be modified and rebuilt without the danger of data loss.

Data Maturity Models

Organizations inevitably follow a basic progression in the use of data over time. They begin by digitizing nondigital assets, proceed to store and organize data more efficiently, and eventually centralize and link up databases across the enterprise. Reporting is implemented and improves as more high-quality data becomes available. The data recorded and stored throughout this process is eventually useful for applications requiring larger amounts of data and more sophisticated processing such as forecasting, analytics, and machine learning exercises.

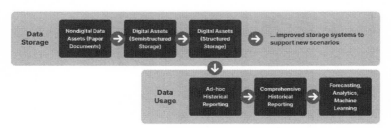

It can be difficult to quantify and comprehend where an organization is in this process. As a result, various so-called "maturity models" have been suggested which attempt to provide a classification system for understanding the state of a set of systems under consideration. Most maturity models include four to six categories that reflect the progression above. Each category includes representative tools or uses of data that an organization must be capable of to be considered a member.

There are different designations that might be used such as data "aware," "reactive," "proficient," or "driven." Employee classifications might be mapped to each category, such as business analyst, data operations, data analyst, or data scientist. Other areas of data management can be mapped to the categories. For instance, data quality in less mature organizations will be poor and include "noisy" data that is inconsistent and difficult to retrieve, whereas data in mature organizations will be high-quality, consistent, and readily available.

Orbweaver Perspective: Platforms

Many companies are dependent on good data, but face daunting challenges to establish a comprehensive data architecture and policies across the organization. Often these are due to staffing issues or political challenges. Partner SaaS platforms, such as those offered by Orbweaver, assume a huge burden that goes beyond the day-to-day operation of a system. They embed a huge amount of analysis and design expertise along with hard-wrought lessons learned. The buy-versus-build decision is often well worth the effort due to the assurance of the ability to – almost immediately – be operating at parity with competitors using the platform, without a substantial time investment upfront.

Conclusion

The value of data is realized when people—skilled users—are able to acquire information to make good decisions that derive value for the company. An understanding of users and what information they need is vital. The form that they can best consume information—reports, charts, visualizations, and power-user query tools, for example—is also important. The way they need to communicate and share the data is essential. The tools provided must allow users to customize and share data and ideally discourage the standard fallback of spreadsheets, which are challenging to manage, audit, and control. Digital transformation needs to keep people in view, but the underlying systems and storage are the raw materials applied to bring about required change in modern organizations.

9

Assessing and Monitoring Risk

Risk Management Process

Risk is unavoidable. Businesses that refuse to enact and embrace change risk missing opportunities that emerge from changing market conditions. Essentially, they cease to improve. Growth involves change, and change involves risk. Accepting this reality is essential for professionals whose livelihood depends on the ability to identify and mitigate risk. Change is also liberating, highlighting occasions to improve business areas and respond innovatively to customer demands and market conditions.

Digital transformation projects are exciting opportunities for positive change, which must be researched and managed. While stakeholders tend to discuss tangible positive outcomes and the systems used to achieve these goals, risk management is also essential throughout the process.

Risk management involves focused attention on types of risk, quantification of their potential impact, and a continuous auditing process. Risks must be identified, analyzed, monitored, prioritized, and mitigated when possible. The process is ongoing and iterative, so new and better information can be incorporated as it becomes available.

Responses to risk can be categorized into two general categories: remediation and mitigation. Remediation occurs when a threat can be eradicated altogether. Mitigation is essentially damage control, minimizing or deferring effects that cannot be eliminated.

As risks are identified, they can be cataloged and organized into groupings summarized to provide a broader profile. As identified risks are analyzed, mitigation potential becomes better understood, and responsible parties can be consulted to understand and quantify the likelihood of the risk becoming a reality and the effects of its impact. This analysis also will naturally entail remediation or mitigation possibilities. At this point, there is a reasonable understanding of the broad set of concerns in view, and monitoring can commence. This involves revisiting identified risks and updating related metrics to maintain a current view and provide data that can be used to detect historical trends in each area. Information gleaned from monitoring informs the prioritization of risk mitigation and remediation efforts. From here, an actual response can be implemented—either mitigating or remediating the risk. This chapter will focus on the first and last steps in this process.

	Description
Identify	Determine and categorize specific areas of risk.
Analyze	Describe the nature of each risk. Specify its probability of occurring, severity, and the cost/effort to remediate it. Define metrics to quantify each risk objectively.
Monitor	Observe, collect metric data, and track identified risks. Note trends on data collected over time.
Prioritize	Prioritize risk mitigation and remediation where applicable.
Mitigate	Respond to risk where possible. Implement risk mitigation (or remediation). Revisit earlier steps in the process.

Areas of Risk

Risks can be challenging to identify. Even the most dangerous threat can remain invisible until an event occurs. Considering broad risk categories can help keep potential areas of concern in clear view. Doing so is the precursor to initiating a quick and effective response. The ability to respond to a risk effectively has a significant effect on the quantifiable seriousness of the event's impact. The categorizations below, while overlapping and somewhat limited, address areas that may be significantly impacted or under threat. Keep in mind, it's impossible to identify every possible problem that may occur.

Areas of Risk Management

Strategy
Technology
Operations
Project Management
Finance
Regulations
Security
Individual

Strategic risks surface when a project deviates from the organization's overall goals or objectives. Strategic risks are particularly dangerous because of their incongruence with business goals. Strategic failures result from ineffective monitoring and directing of work effort. Thankfully, strategic risks are easy to address through proper project management. A related concern at the strategic level is competitive risk. While digital transformation is risky for any enterprise, it is riskier to avoid transformation altogether. Lower-level management and workers outside the competitive landscape must rely on strategic plans to account for business competitors' activities.

Technology

Technical problems, failures, or suboptimal outcomes are rarely restricted to computers and software. They are usually the result of human beings misunderstanding, misapplying, or mismanaging these resources. That said, these "people problems" clearly manifest themselves as created processes or systems that experience a failure of some sort. An obvious risk is systems being unavailable due to crashes, network disruption, unavailability of dependent services, or security compromises. Data loss may or may not be visible, but depending on the nature of the data, this can be devastating. Subtle failures that can lead to increased security risk often occur as a result of insufficient monitoring of software component versions and accompanying upgrades. With changes being rolled out as part of an enterprise project, unidentified development failures can result in bad releases.

Technology failures are a well understood domain and have inspired standard processes, including software development life cycle, code scans, continuous integration, and quality assurance testing. These practices, along with architectural best practices oversight and organizational disciplines like backup methodologies, disaster recovery, and security auditing, limit the risk inherent in complex technical projects. These processes and practices are firmly established and well-refined in software organizations, but tend to be sporadically implemented in companies where software is not a core competency. Risk mitigation outside of a company's core competency is a primary reason for collaborating with specialists outside the organization.

Methods of responding to engineering risks include the following items, ordered by increasing seriousness:[48]

- Technical and management reviews of the engineering process (revised design),

48 Kossiakoff, A. and W.N. Sweet, 2003, Systems Engineering Principles and Practice, John Wiley and Sons, Inc., pp. 98-106

- Oversight of designated component engineering (system focus),

- Analysis and testing of critical design assets (QA process),

- Rapid prototyping and test feedback (validation via exploratory prototype),

- Consideration of relieving critical design requirements (revising project scope), and

- Fallback/parallel developments.

Operations

Operational risk can overlap significantly with technical risk, but tends to be associated with manual interventions by operational staff having an adverse effect. Risks in this area directly impact the production system, but are distinguished from technology risks that tend to focus on non-functional, incidental complexity in the system. For instance, an administrative user could inadvertently erase a large amount of data. An essential system could be mistakenly shut down in the middle of a load process. Data intended for one location could be stored in another. Mistakes in authorization configuration can result in a violation of security policies.

Operational risk can be mitigated through clearly defined processes and aggressive auditing. Failures continue to occur because clearly defined processes are often not remembered or followed correctly when they involve many separate steps. Wherever there are manual steps in a business process performed by several individuals, there is a significant chance of failure. The extent of the damage varies considerably.

Operational risk can be eliminated in some instances by providing software-based automation validation and system design that prevents certain errors. Again, the topic of affordance becomes relevant as it represents actions available via the systems and processes to an individual actor. This is an opportunity for digital transformation to be a positive force in improving user experience and the experience of other parties, including the support of IT personnel, who are less likely to have their day disrupted by an operational disaster.

Project Management

Project managers exist because of the inevitable risk accompanying organizational change at an enterprise scale. Risks like inaccurate estimates, changes in requirements, and project scope modifications can impact the delivery date. These risks can also affect the actual or perceived quality of a deliverable. Perceived quality can further be impacted by communication issues, inaccurate stakeholder expectations, or poor documentation. Project management risks encompass other areas, including strategic concerns (lack of commitment to a project), technical challenges (visible as famous "death marches" materializing as long hours to achieve near-impossible goals), and operational problems (failure to educate operations staff on proper operation of new or upgraded software).

Entire books describe generally applicable project management practices that ensure success. In practice, there are two primary components for ensuring project success: managers who have a track record of successful deliverables in a domain, and a team of participants who operate well with that manager. Past performance is not a sure predictor of future success, but it is one of the best estimators available. While not a popular opinion, it's worth considering in light of an over-reliance on professional certifications to demonstrate project management acumen.

Finances

The business of business is to make money, so financial risk is generally tracked with intense scrutiny. Standard business practices like establishing budgets and tracking costs apply to digital transformation projects just like any other. Accurate predictions generally exist in well-understood domains where the cycle of estimation and analysis of outcome have occurred many times. Financial shortfalls are more likely when working in an unfamiliar domain.

One example that drifts into a technology concern is estimating cloud expenses. It is notoriously challenging to obtain accurate estimates of costs when running services in AWS, Microsoft Azure, or Google Cloud. Organizations generally have to work with these services for a period of time to get a baseline for costs, identify areas for savings, and optimize their usage. Organizations with a history of running servers in data centers frequently emulate the design with a cloud provider. This "lift-and-shift" pattern has operational value in that it maintains parity with previous experience, but it is generally not the best way to derive value using cloud resources.

Regulations

The electronics industry has specific risk concerns related to regulatory restrictions, which vary based on the jurisdiction and customer involved. The U.S. Federal Government has laws regulating government contractors and particular agencies, as well as the military to enforce additional rules. European Union (EU) regulations address social and environmental concerns, and NATO regulates business practices in a manner similar to the U.S. military.

EU regulations that address environmental concerns include the Restriction of Hazardous Substances (RoHS) Directive, which restricts the use of lead, cadmium, mercury, and other substances in electronics equipment. Registration, Evaluation, Authorization, and Restriction of Chemicals (REACH), an EU regulation, also addresses the environment and the protection of human health. Waste from Electrical and Electronic

Equipment (WEEE) promotes sustainable production and consumption of these items. Regulations that address the well-being of people extend beyond pure environmental concerns and include rules related to the prohibition of human trafficking issued by the Federal Acquisition Regulation (FAR) Council and the Department of Defense (DOD).

Military compliance is required by International Traffic in Arms Regulations (ITAR) and Export Administration Regulations (EAR), which regulate defense-related technologies. Counterfeit parts are also a concern, resulting in an amendment (Section 818) to the 2012 National Defense Authorization Act that requires the DOD, as well as its contractors and subcontractors, to detect and weed out high-risk suppliers to protect the supply chain for imported electronic parts.

Regulation can also overlap with other risk areas, including technology and project management. Quality management compliance standards that might affect a company include ISO-9001-2015, ISO-13485-2016, and UL/CSA. The response to regulatory risk is compliance, with legal activity generally handled day to day by dedicated professionals in the industry. Involving the right people early in the process and when questions arise generally keeps projects from encountering problems in this area.

Although not a regulatory concern, reputational risk is also worthy of consideration. Companies spend millions of dollars building a brand and creating a marketing image. Failed projects that impact end users can cause serious damage, even if no specific regulatory rule is violated.

Security (Cyber) Risk

While security breaches steal headlines, breaches that have occurred but have not been identified are more troubling. Unauthorized access and use of systems can result in the leaking of private data. Data can be intercepted in networks that are not adequately secured. Data can be obtained outside of applications by hackers who gain access to a server through some obscure, unexpected path. The damage caused by security breaches can be substantial and have a significant financial impact. Cyber insurance policies specifically designed to cover a business's liability for a data breach involving sensitive information offer support.

A key concern related to security risk—and technological risk in general—is a team's ability to respond to a problem when it occurs. A fast response time can help contain damage, limit the blast radius, and prevent additional exposure. This requires a set of professionals with the ability and authority to act quickly when an event occurs. The traditional segregation into business silos within many organizations is at odds with the broad organization's need to respond decisively and globally when addressing an issue.

Individual Risk

In one sense, any failure in any area of risk management affects people. However, some failures that do not fall neatly into the above-mentioned categories can affect individuals profoundly. For example, a botched translation in a business application could prove offensive to an end user, but might not fit into a category. As in other areas of digital transformation, it is always important to keep the audience of users and system participants in mind when identifying areas of concern.

Various people can cause failures, and the definition of a perceived failure might differ depending on a person's role. A customer can both cause a failure and be a significant audience to other failures. On the other hand, an employee (an internal customer) has a different level of access which may translate into a more significant amount of concern or contribute to worse failures. Likewise, third parties and investors can be the causes or recipients of damage. Traditional businesses need to leverage various forms of global communications, including social media, to maintain positive messaging and brand associations addressed to a global audience. Considering the unique viewpoints of those contributing to, or affected by, risk is immensely valuable toward proactively identifying organizational risks.

Risk Mitigation

Risk mitigation efforts are tailored to the specific area of concern. Common strategies for reacting to risk include remediation, avoidance, acceptance, control, or transfer of risk.

Strategy	Description
Remediate	Make a fix or change that prevents the risk from materializing.
Avoid	Similar to remediation, but it doesn't necessarily fix the problem; instead, it defers or side-steps it.
Accept	Assume the risk, but make no attempt to mitigate it.
Control	Attempt to change a risk, create a buffer, or otherwise reduce the risk or its effects.
Transfer	Externalize risk by assigning it to another party or sharing the risk with a partner.
Monitor	This strategy is often coupled with others. It involves acknowledging risk and establishing metrics to determine the probability of an incident and the potential damage that would result.

Various pithy slogans have gained popularity among programmers and data scientists that highlight risks to avoid or aspiring best practices. These "rules of thumb" are cited and explained below.

Rules of Thumb

View Situations from Multiple Perspectives

"Premature optimization is the root of all evil." This quote by Tony Hoare, popularized by Donald Knuth, points out that trying to improve performance too early can be futile.

In a more general sense, optimization via focusing on one area at the expense of all others is also a concern. For instance, reducing the number of servers in use to a bare minimum makes no allowance for the redundancy required for high levels of availability or disaster recovery. There is a need for balance. For example, processes need to be formalized sufficiently to codify business activity into a standard manner of working. Processes also need to provide transparency into what is being done and build flexibility for adjustments. Both formalism and flexibility are required in an effective system.

Based on this saying, the general risk to avoid is a myopic, narrow-minded focus on only one part of a project. Team members will tend to specialize in one perspective or another, but must keep all in view. This risk is also at play in the following adage.

Trade-offs

"Fast, cheap, good. Pick two." This project management saying highlights the fact that engineering is about trade-offs.

Increasing resources in one area results in a corresponding decrease in one or both of the other areas.

Accept the reality that actions have corresponding reactions. Attempt to be realistic when making decisions that affect one person/team/area and recognize that attention will be diverted from other areas.

Abstractions

The aphorism "all models are wrong, but some are useful" is often attributed to statistician George Box. The truth is that any model or abstraction captures only part of its corresponding reality or the total body of data available. As such, it can never be completely accurate. However, if a model is well constructed or an abstraction well designed, it is adequate for practical uses despite being incomplete or inaccurate.

The clear risk corresponding to this saying is that it is very easy to create models or extractions that are *not* useful. They may capture a large amount of information, but that information might not be relevant to the problem that needs to be solved. A focus on solving a specific problem and concretely validating system behavior and processes is far more valuable than failing to describe a running system with flashy presentations and orderly diagrams.

Clear Definitions

"There are only two hard things in computer science: cache invalidation and naming things." This maxim by Phil Karlton has inspired a host of variations.[49] The main points in this phrase highlight nomenclature and maintaining data in several locations.

The habit of naming things like parts of a system, releases, and other internal terminology used within teams is fraught with

---

49 https://martinfowler.com/bliki/TwoHardThings.html

Orbweaver Perspective: Technical Focus

CTO Tony Powell stated the following: "Orbweaver was born from two industries: contract manufacturing within the electronics industry and large-scale technical engagements related to data automation. Orbweaver's core value proposition is our expertise in moving very large amounts of data, normalizing that data, and securely transporting it between two trading partners. We are also adept at unfettering data stores from systems or DBs that were previously monolithic in terms of connectivity within an organization's digital platform—meaning they were inaccessible and disconnected. Today, we move data related to about a billion transactions per month, and that number increases every day. Most big distributors are our clients, or we move their data on behalf of mutual trading partners. Our technical expertise has demonstrably provided tremendous value to organizations that are able to maintain their primary focus on their core company mission."

problems. The natural drift in language use—and of software systems— unavoidably leads to some amount of obscurity over time. Glossaries can help in some cases. Maintaining separate but mapped, internal and external release versions can also help prevent confusion.

Cache invalidation is a specific technical problem used to provide better performance while avoiding the presentation of stale, out-of-date data. The more general principle addresses storing data in multiple locations. Make sure the canonical version of data is well understood and balances performance and data storage.

The general area of risk addressed in this statement is the need for effective ongoing communication. Projects that cease to maintain communication are in danger of veering off course.

Affordance Effects

Conway's law[50] states: "Organizations design systems that mirror their own communication structure." Digital transformation is squarely positioned to offset problems in earlier systems caused by this tendency.

This is a negative example of affordance. The risks in this area have been discussed already because they are so impactful.

Unavoidable Grunt Work

Data scientists spend a significant amount of their time—anywhere from 60% to 80%—cleaning data. This often-bantered, pseudo-statistic rings true to anyone who has dealt with a substantial data project. The data is often not clean, normalized, linked, or in a remotely usable form. An enormous amount of up-front effort must be expended before business objectives come into play.

The more general risk is related to "un-fun" work. During system design, think beyond the "happy path." Failures can and will happen. Design—particularly of new systems—tends to focus on the most common successful processes that match the way the system is intended to be used. The excitement of creating a new system can divert attention from serious concerns that are more mundane or irritating.

Remember, building a system is only the first step. Over time, support costs will exceed the initial investment in a system. And even a perfectly designed system will need to be changed and updated because the world is dynamic and ever-changing.

---

50 https://en.wikipedia.org/wiki/Conway%27s_law

Right People in the Right Place

Not every person is comfortable in every stage of a system's life. The "Pioneer, Settler, and Town Planner Strategy Cycle"[51] views the three categories as types of teams (or individuals with specific skills) that are active in a system or project at a given time. Pioneers thrive in the unstructured, early stages of design. Settlers pick up where the pioneers leave off, fleshing out incomplete work. Town planners adopt the stable system from the settlers, then scale and optimize it.

DevOps Paradigm Shift

Two DevOps sayings bear mentioning: "cattle not sheep" and "configuration as code." The former expresses the nature of cloud computing where server resources are not manually created as unique, custom "snowflakes." Instead, automation is used to build virtual machines or containers that accomplish work that would have been done by manually built servers in the past. This type of automation requires discipline and the creation of resources expressed in the second saying, "configuration as code". All of the resources needed to create virtual servers must be maintained in version control and subject to an SDLC, just like any other piece of software. Organizations often attempt to partially adopt modern DevOps practices and end up with technical debt. The new DevOps automation is incomplete and error-prone, and the old legacy maintenance of servers is not accounted for in newer automation.

We Don't Know What We Don't Know

Variations of "it is difficult to predict, especially the future" have been attributed to everyone from Yogi Berra to Mark Twain to Nobel Prize-winning physicist Niels Bohr. Nassim

---

51 https://interaction.net.au/articles/
pioneers-settlers-town-planners-how-innovation-works/

N. Taleb also has written several books discussing "black swans"--unpredictable events defying normal expectations that have potentially severe consequences. He and his co-authors emphasize human limitation and the inability to make accurate predictions about significant events, as follows: "Instead of trying to anticipate low-probability, high-impact events, we should reduce our vulnerability to them. Risk management, we believe, should entail lessening the impact of what we don't understand—not futile attempts to develop sophisticated techniques and stories that perpetuate our illusions of being able to understand and predict the social and economic environment."[52]

Conclusion

New opportunities often generate excitement for businesses, while failures and threats can bring destruction. Risks, which may originate internally or from external sources, can be remediated, mitigated, or prevented. Quantifying risk is difficult, and organizational biases inevitably inhibit our ability to discuss such challenges openly. "Risk mitigation is painful, not a natural act for humans to perform," said Gentry Lee, chief systems engineer at JPL, a division of NASA.[53] Preparation is essential to react effectively to failure when it occurs. The additional effort and planning that addresses risk are essential to any digital transformation project.

---

52 https://hbr.org/2009/10/
the-six-mistakes-executives-make-in-risk-management
53 https://hbr.org/2012/06/managing-risks-a-new-frame-
work#:~:text=Effective%20risk%2Dmanagement%20processes%20
must,National%20Aeronautics%20and%20Space%20Administration.

10

Technical Trends

Both near-term events and the progressive development of platforms help drive trends in technology. Near-term events include headline-grabbing news about market demands, cybersecurity events, supply chain disruptions, pandemics, geopolitical instability, and similar changes and concerns. Progressive development of platforms occurs as a result of anticipating and taking the next logical step in an area that provides an improved end-user experience.

The response to near-term events is evident to people doing business and mandating targeted responses. The COVID-19 pandemic drove telecommuting and made remote work a practical necessity. Shortages of electronic components drove demand for technologies that make it possible to quickly find and procure alternatives. Disruptions in the supply chain have resulted in increased spending on technologies and platforms that provide greater visibility and resilience. These trends are not driven by technology but require a response that leverages it.

Another interplay between near-term and progressive development involves improvements in technology that tend to reach a tipping point where technologies that previously were not cost-effective or practical become so. This can result in a situation where early adopters "win," triggering a near-term event where competitors play catch-up. To monitor and identify such tipping points, slow-moving trends are worth tracking.

Noteworthy industry innovation is ongoing, but it's challenging to remain well informed while focusing on company-specific objectives. Fortunately, there are a number of relatively impartial sources for tracking technical trends. Two sources described below, Gartner and O'Reilly Media, provide a helpful perspective on how to interpret changes in technology. Each group has a different focus and audience, highlighting trends that fit under the digital transformation umbrella.

Top Strategic Technology Trends for 2022

Gartner identified the top 12 strategic technology trends for 2022.[54] While these seem to fall into the "next logical step" category, spending in a given area will be influenced by near-term events that are fresh on managers' minds. As these trends are strategic, they can be understood within the context of digital transformation. Many of these trends are not brand-new technology projects but incremental improvements that can be folded into ongoing initiatives for organizational transformation.

The incremental nature of these trends is evident in the descriptions below: flexible, resilient, composable, elastic, agile, rapid, disciplined, streamlined, as well as the actions noted like improve, build out, and integrate. These terms all

---

54   https://www.gartner.com/en/information-technology/insights/top-technology-trends

imply some area of already-existing functionality that is in some way changed, augmented, or perhaps transformed in a manner that makes the organization's services more effective.

	Trend	Description
1	Data Fabric	Flexible, resilient integration of data sources across platforms and business users
2	Cybersecurity Mesh	Flexible, composable architecture that integrates widely distributed and disparate security services
3	Privacy-Enhancing Computation	Secures the processing of personal data in untrusted environments
4	Cloud-Native Platforms	Architectures that are resilient, elastic, and agile, enabling rapid response to digital change (rather than lift-and-shift)
5	Composable Applications	Composable applications built from business-centric modular components
6	Decision Intelligence	Modeling a decision as a set of processes, using intelligence and analytics to inform, learn from, and refine decisions
7	Hyperautomation	A disciplined, business-driven approach to rapidly identify, vet, and automate as many business and IT processes as possible
8	AI Engineering	Automates updates to data, models, and applications to streamline AI delivery
9	Distributed Enterprises	Digital-first, remote-first business model to improve employee experiences, digitalize consumer and partner touchpoints, and build out product experiences

10	Total Experience	A business strategy that integrates employee, customer, and user experience across multiple touchpoints to accelerate growth
11	Autonomic Systems	Self-managed physical or software systems that learn from their environments and dynamically modify their algorithms in real-time to optimize their behavior in complex ecosystems
12	Generative AI	Create new content similar to an original without directly copying it

O'Reilly Radar

O'Reilly Media Inc. provides monthly reports that track technology and business trends deemed important or interesting.[55] O'Reilly is a media publisher and relies on technical practitioners for its content. This enables a unique perspective tied to a particularly innovative subculture within the tech industry. At the time of this writing, sections of their site[56] include everything from articles about specific software packages to social changes affecting businesses.

Section	*Description*
AI/ML	Artificial intelligence and machine learning

---

55 https://www.oreilly.com/radar/topics/radar-trends/
56 https://www.oreilly.com/radar/

Future of the Firm	Organizational structures, payment schemes, and changing expectations, skills, and tools
Innovation and Disruption	Emerging tools, trends, issues, and context
Next Architecture	Cloud and next-generation architectures
Next Economy	Balancing people and automation

Again, words like "future," "innovation," and "next" in the sections above highlight the incremental building of new solutions on a set of existing technologies. And even seemingly new technologies like AI/ML require an infrastructure and data that has been built up over time.

Within the O'Reilly Radar, categories are observations related to security and privacy, connected hardware (IoT), augmented reality, infrastructure and operations, programming, robotics, ethics, law and legislation, and more esoteric topics like quantum computing. There is a wealth of detailed, current analysis on specific technologies being leveraged to create actual business solutions. There is also helpful guidance about certain overhyped technologies that have no clear path to realization.

Practices

DevOps (and Other Ops)

One way of understanding the DevOps methodology is to consider the composition of teams. Silo fragmentation has occurred as a result of technology segmentation and specialization. Silos of developers, IT operations, security, and other departments develop misaligned objectives that damage an organization's ability to implement changes. Creating teams with several of these roles combined can improve this situation. DevOps involves teams with both developer and operational responsibilities. Similarly, SecOps aims to automate security tasks by combining security and IT operations teams. DevSecOps adds developers to this heterogeneous group. The most effective groups have some members with a deep level of experience in one or more of the areas, though there is generally some degree of specialization among members.

Another way of understanding DevOps is considering what each group contributes to the software development process. Developers have certain knowledge about how the system works that will go over the heads of operations staff. In addition, developers tend to proactively create automation as part of their work, where traditional IT operations employees tend to be more reactive. When developers are faced with certain operations tasks, they can develop (more) software that follows a relatively rigorous process. On the other hand, IT operations staff tends to be more familiar with manual interventions.

Most established, non-tech companies are dominated by IT operations staff rather than software developers. They often do not have the budget, skills, tools, or culture to establish DevOps teams and practices that derive any value or benefit. The best path forward is to encourage and grow internal staff, while augmenting the organization with technical partners who focus on these practices, freeing internal staff to address ongoing support concerns.

Specific Technologies

Having considered broad strategic concerns, this chapter will conclude with a closer look at the technical reality behind some of the technologies that have recently received a great deal of attention.

Artificial Intelligence

A citation from a well-respected 2003 book on AI indicates that the discipline has been around for more than 50 years. This history[57] is remarkable given the common perception that advances in this area only occurred in the last few years.

"AI is one of the newest sciences. Work started soon after World War II, and the name itself was coined in 1956...AI currently encompasses a huge variety of subfields, ranging from general purpose areas, such as learning and perception, to such specific tasks as playing chess, proving mathematical theorems, writing poetry, and diagnosing diseases. AI systematizes and automates intellectual tasks and is, therefore, potentially relevant to any sphere of human intellectual activity. In this sense, it is a truly universal field."[58]

There is a great deal of overlap between "systematizes and automates intellectual tasks" and digital transformation. The term AI helpfully provides a category for discussion without identifying a specific technology or platform. Recently, many uses of AI refer to the specific area of machine learning (ML).

Machine Learning (ML)

Traditional development involves a programmer implementing an algorithm that reads data and produces an output. Machine learning involves building a model from data that is used to produce an output. There are many ways of categorizing techniques in use—differentiating 14 or more types

---

57 https://sitn.hms.harvard.edu/flash/2017/
history-artificial-intelligence/
58 Stuart J. Russel and Peter Norvig, Artificial Intelligence A Modern Approach, Second Edition. (New Jersey: Pearson Education Inc, 2003), p 1.

of ML[59]—but most are variations of those represented in the following chart. In fact, most tasks are a specific type of ML known as supervised learning, which reads a set of data and makes a prediction based on this data.

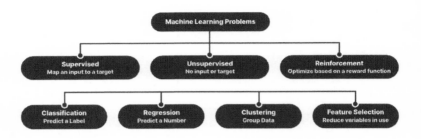

The diagram lists a few other dominant categories of ML in use today. Machine learning has achieved impressive results in image classification, natural language processing (NLP), customer churn prediction, and other areas. To understand how ML can be applied, consider that Apple has created a developer tool to create ML models usable on their platform quickly. The available templates suggest a number of tangible applications where ML might be of use:

- Image classification: Classify the dominant object or scene in an image.

- Object detection: Locate and classify different types of objects in an image.

- Style transfer: Transform an image or video to adopt the visual style of a reference image.

- Hand post classification: Classify a hand pose in an image.

---

59 https://machinelearningmastery.com/
types-of-learning-in-machine-learning/

- Action classification: Classify a person's action in a video clip based on his/her body movement.

- Hand action classification: Classify a hand gesture in a video clip based on the fingers and hand movement.

- Activity classification: Classify the dominant activity captured in motion sensor data.

- Sound classification: Classify the dominant sound in an audio clip.

- Text classification: Classify the dominant topic, theme, or sentiment in natural language text.

- Word tagging: Split natural language text into a classified phrase or word tokens based on their contextual roles.

- Tabular classification: Predict the categorical value of a feature given other features' values. Features are represented as columns in tabular data.

- Tabular regression: Predict the numeric value of a feature given other features' values. Features are represented as columns in tabular data.

- Recommendation: Recommend new items given to others based on how often users interact with or rate them together.

Notice the number of times the word "classification" is used in the templates listed above. These are all examples of supervised classification. What differs is the input used to make a prediction. Because a sound, video, picture, and set of words can all be represented digitally, models can be built based on labeled training data which allow a model to make a prediction on an input not previously seen.

Many different ML models exist. Picture a scatter plot with the x-axis representing height and the y-axis representing weight and height of American basketball andfootball players. A simple model might simply divide the problem space using a line (linear model).

The model would then make predictions that one side of the line represents football players, while the other represents basketball players. The practical effect might seem like magic until it is pushed too far. For example, the model only has two categories. Despite much additional evidence indicating that a new data point represents a hockey player, the model will predict either a football or basketball player. The model also would predict one of these two categories when data is obviously invalid, for example, if the input indicated a human with a height of a kilometer or having a negative weight.

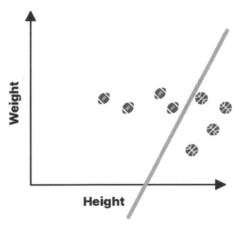

This model is very simple. It considers only two "dimensions" (height and weight) and divides the problem space with a straight line. It is also very easy to visualize and understand. More sophisticated models can be built to consider a larger number of dimensions and non-linear divisions of the problem space. These models tend to be more difficult to interpret, which makes it harder to explain why the model made a specified prediction.

Neural Networks

A neural network often addressed under the term "deep learning" is a type of system that can be used for certain types of supervised classification problems. Neural networks have been around for years, but they recently gained attention due to discoveries and applications resulting in the best-performing AI systems developed to date, including speech recognition, Google translate, facial recognition, and computer vision applications.

Assessment

AI has obvious applicability for electronics sourcing, procurement, and manufacturing. Nearly any digital transformation process arguably encapsulates and automates a process in an intelligent way. ML also has fascinating implications for the electronic industry. Being able to dynamically classify parts, predict supply chain disruptions, optimize logistics, or predict demand for a given part are areas for application. Implementing projects in these areas should be approached cautiously for the following reasons:

- Good models require good data—and lots of it. Without a large volume of high-quality data, it is difficult to build a useful mode. Even if a large volume of high-quality data is available, the data will need to be transformed in various ways to be ingested into the model for predictions. The earlier emphasis in this book on database and API development provides the foundation for good data and subsequent ML work.

- Models need to be updated as data changes. There is a tendency for practitioners to build a model once and expect it to work well into the future. This may be possible when the represented data does not change much, for example, in facial recognition, where human faces have certain common characteristics and proportions that do not change significantly over time. However, economic activity varies greatly, and many innovations impacting the use of electronic parts are surprising and simply not represented in historical data.

- Models need to be deployed. A model running on a data scientist's laptop works for demos but not general usage. The deployment of models involves a set of skills and technologies unfamiliar to many who build the models. An entire new "Ops," machine learning ops or MLops, has emerged to address this concern—along with cloud offerings like AWS ML Ops and SageMaker—to make models available to a wider audience. Related to the previous point, deployment is not a one-time activity. Updated models must be built and deployed using a pipeline approximating a traditional SDLC.

- Sophisticated models are difficult to explain. Certain simple models are easy to explain. We considered linear models earlier. A decision tree that describes a set of if/else statements used to arrive at a conclusion is similarly explainable. Sophisticated models are complicated to explain. If there is an expectation that a prediction not simply be given, but an explanation also be provided, ML may not be the correct approach.

- Model quality can be challenging to evaluate. Care must be taken when training and testing models. One standard approach involves splitting data into training and test sets, never mingling the two. This avoids problems with "overfitting," which occurs when a model essentially just memorizes a test set but does not derive usable patterns that can be applied to new data inputs. At times, a model will work well with the data provided initially, but the data used when the model is deployed differs in a significant way, rendering the model ineffective.

Despite these cautions, it is worth investigating AI/ML projects with defined scope. An immense amount is learned in the process about data availability and quality, even if the project does not produce immediately useful, seemingly "magic" predictions. Data validation, cleansing, and transformation can benefit existing reporting and analytics. The activity and attention generated in a project of this type help pave the way for process improvements that provide residual benefits beyond the specified goal.

Blockchain

Bitcoin and other cryptocurrencies have made headlines, along with new types of virtual assets such as non-fungible tokens (NFTs). These are certainly an economic phenomena and an interesting application of technologies that seek to provide a decentralized, zero-trust, transparent system for data and economic transactions. The sheer publicity related to this area has forced businesses to consider the possibility of these technologies disrupting existing businesses. In addition, the size and scale of these networks might also suggest new technologies that can be applied in the business world. This is a rapidly changing area but foundationally relies on a few basic technologies: distributed ledgers and security/cryptography.

A blockchain is a type of distributed ledger. "Distributed" indicates that a single distributed ledger runs on different machines. The term "ledger" indicates that activities are recorded in an auditable fashion as a series of transactions recording each change, much like an accountant's ledger. When implemented by cryptocurrencies, transactions include cryptographic hashing to ensure message security and maintain the validity of the blockchain. Special algorithms (proof of work for Bitcoin; proof of stake in newer blockchains) are used in the process to ensure that participants cannot compromise the integrity of the stored data. The distributed nature of the technology has captured the imagination of many and led to the term "web3," describing a decentralized evolution of the web built on blockchain technology. The term "metaverse" tends to be conflated with web3 but is focused more on virtual reality and immersive experiences. Both web3 and the metaverse are visions of a new, improved internet, but they are not necessarily dependent.

Assessment

There are several interesting ideas related to distributed ledgers, but a great deal of hype obscures their actual value. There are solutions pertaining to trust and identity beneath the surface, but they have not been clearly mapped to existing problems at this point. This is an area to monitor, but any projects in this space should be considered highly speculative.[60] A few concerns include:

---

60 https://www.oreilly.com/radar/
why-its-too-early-to-get-excited-about-web3/

Orbweaver Perspective: Processes

CTO Tony Powell describes how companies benefit from Orbweaver's DevOps processes: "Electronics manufacturing companies are implementing business process automation solutions like the Orbweaver platform, to increase efficiency, reduce errors, and integrate data into a single, useful system to improve information and communication throughout the organization and remain competitive in a rapidly changing industry.

Orbweaver simplifies internal processes for electronics manufacturing by integrating our partners directly with their suppliers and customers to eliminate common data management challenges such as RFQ intake, price book management, and PO issuance to save time and money. Companies focus on their core competencies while advancing their digital capabilities built on our modern technology stack and processes, which include a robust SDLC and integrated DevOps."

- Established businesses are unwilling to give up data privacy. Certain blockchain initiatives are suggested to replace private authorities that own data. Businesses have little motivation—and many deterrents—for giving up existing data. So despite the fact that a number of private blockchain projects exist, they are not experiencing widespread use.

- People prefer to trust authorities. Despite problems with central authorities misusing and mismanaging private data, most people do not have the time or inclination to manage their resources. Social media platforms consistently demonstrate the willingness of a growing sector of the population to share information about themselves rather indiscriminately. Data breaches at the highest levels have had little impact on the daily behavior of the average consumer. For all of human history, middlemen have provided a buffering effect even in non-technical realms. It seems more likely that an effective business solution that includes decentralization as a "value-add" would be more likely to succeed.

- Public blockchains lack transparency. The intent of "leveling the playing field" by promoting transparency is laudable. The current tooling makes viewing the state of a blockchain challenging even for experienced users. This is a technical problem that will become less of a concern over time.

Blockchain is both a technical and a social/economic phenomenon. The technical maturity of these systems does not warrant investment and usage at this point for most businesses. The social and economic effects are interesting and worth monitoring. The activity and attention in this area make it an almost inevitable area of interest. Still, there is no real call for dedicated action without a very specialized—and likely speculative—plan.

Virtualization (Containerization/Orchestration)

Computers used to be primarily thought of as physical pieces of hardware. Virtualization—or the creation of software to emulate hardware—has been around for decades, but had a resurgence with companies like VMWare in the 1990s. Early cloud providers created virtual machine offerings like Amazon EC2[61] instances. This type of virtualization maintained a fairly close mapping between physical and software-based machines. Virtualization remains in wide use today, as does the original paradigm of physical machines in data centers.

---

61 https://aws.amazon.com/ec2/

Linux Containers (LXC)[62] were developed in 2008. This "lightweight virtualization" provides namespace isolation for processes and resources while using the host machine's kernel. Docker was built on this technology and provided a convenient way of packaging applications and running sets of applications on a single machine that previously required separate machines. Docker distinguishes between images (deployment templates) and containers (running instances). Images are hosted in registries. Servers with connections to these registries can download images and create one or more instances of running containers.

Cloud providers offer services where images can be stored, and containers can be run. Docker Hub, Amazon Elastic Container Registry (ECR), Azure Container Registry, and Google Container Registry can host docker images. Amazon Elastic Container Service (ECS), Fargate, Azure Container Instances, and similar services provide ready-made services that can host-run containers.

The ability to easily deploy and create docker containers proved to be an effective solution to certain availability and scaling challenges, but created new questions as to how to consistently deploy and orchestrate communication between containers. Kubernetes emerged as the orchestration platform of choice. Along with an ecosystem of related projects, Kubernetes provides a host of flexible platform services allowing deployment and orchestration of containers with a wide range of characteristics. Kubernetes can be hosted on premises and utilized as a cloud service. Amazon Managed Kubernetes Service (EKS), Azure Managed Kubernetes Service (AKS), and Google Kubernetes Engine (GKE) are popular examples of Kubernetes cloud offerings.

---

62 https://linuxcontainers.org/

A sample deployment below using two physical servers, four virtual machines (each hosting a Kubernetes node), four Kubernetes pods, and six docker containers illustrates the multiple levels of orchestration and corresponding complexity implicit to such deployments.

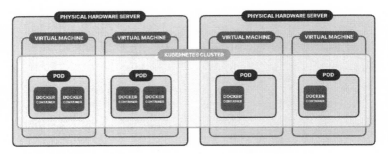

Assessment

Virtualization in all of these forms is a present reality. Technical staff should be comfortable with physical servers, virtual servers, and dockers. Kubernetes is extremely useful and applicable, but requires specialized training that is quite foreign to technologists steeped in traditional system administration practices. Kubernetes tends to also be grouped with modern DevOps practices. Trying to manage Kubernetes clusters using antiquated operational practices will not reap the benefits such systems are designed to provide.

"A virtual machine's behavior must be understood not in isolation but also in relation to a host machine. A performance problem could be due to an issue on the VM itself or on the host machine. Virtualization layers can be nested several layers deep, adding additional complexity. Virtualization removes entire classes of problems, but does require specific technical awareness and know-how to use effectively."[63]

63 Casimir Saternos, Client-Server Web Apps with JavaScript and Java. (Sebasopol California: O'Reilly Media, Inc. 2014), p. 184-185.

There are a wide variety of complex deployment options that mix and match virtualization technologies. Deployments can be on premises in a company data center, cloud-based, or hybrid. Web applications and APIs can run on physical hardware, virtual machines, within containers, or on containers managed by Kubernetes. New systems are designed with these options in mind—two popular architectures that have emerged for cloud-based systems are cloud native and cloud agnostic.

Lift and Shift Vs. Cloud Native

Virtual machines provided by cloud vendors have allowed businesses to migrate servers from corporate data centers to the cloud. This "lift and shift" pattern simply utilizes cloud-based processing and storage rather than maintaining these resources in house. However, mirroring corporate data centers in the cloud is not cost effective when charges are incurred by the hour. It also does not take advantage of the ability to scale and provide resilience using a cloud-specific architecture.

Cloud-native architectures are designed from the ground up to be deployed in a cloud and take advantage of the unique resources available in this environment that cannot be found in legacy data centers. Activities typically performed by internal staff—including migration, configuration, optimization, security, and maintenance—are largely automated by a set of standard tooling.

Assessment

Cloud-native design promises lower costs and better application performance and availability. What's not to like? A complete re-architecture is generally required to enable a legacy system to operate in a cloud-native manner. This type of design is time consuming and risky, and a redesign of an entire system involves data migration, business analysis, and a host of additional resources. In addition, the standardized automation requires a different set of skills and training. Technical staff with modern DevOps skills and a good understanding of virtualization are in a good position to acquire the skills needed to maintain cloud-based resources in a specific environment.

Another risk with a cloud-native approach is a tendency toward vendor lock-in. A system running in AWS might not be able to be ported to Azure or GCP unless specifically designed with this intent. This leads to additional trends toward cloud-agnostic design.

Cloud Agnostic

Cloud vendors have created managed services that mirror specific applications. The following chart illustrates selected popular services available through Amazon.[64]

Application/Service	AWS Equivalent	Open-Source Equivalent
Object Storage	S3	MinIO
Caching	ElastiCache	Redis, Memcached
Queuing		RabbitMQ, Kafka
Relational Database	RDS	MariaDB, PostgresSQL
Graph Database	Neptune	Neo4j
Document Database	Amazon DocumentDB	MongoDB

An AWS-based, cloud-native application can be created to effectively take advantage of these services. Properly

---

64 https://github.com/guenter/aws-oss-alternatives

implemented, the resilient, flexible solution will perform well and be reasonably cost effective. However, if a later decision to migrate the application to Azure or GCP occurred, the effort would be substantial. Despite the fact that major cloud vendors offer equivalent services, they do not operate the same way and the deployment approaches differ.

A solution is to use Kubernetes and ensure all services, such as those listed above, are hosted inside the Kubernetes cluster. The same deployment can then work with any cloud-hosting platform with managed Kubernetes support.

Assessment

A cloud-agnostic approach allows the same cluster to be deployed on premises, in the cloud with any major vendor, and even on a developer's desktop. If a major goal is this kind of portability, there is no better solution available than cloud-agnostic architecture. That said, the cost of a cloud-agnostic solution will differ from a cloud-native solution, and in some cases will be more expensive. A cloud- agnostic solution also requires operations staff to have a deeper understanding of the management of particular services.

In many cases, the best design involves a major portion of a system being created cloud-agnostically, leaving certain data-intensive services like databases to be utilized as vendor-specific managed services. The specific requirements and resources of the application and organization should drive the decision toward a more-or-less cloud-agnostic architecture.

11

Engaging in Transformation

While our book detailing digital transformation is concluding, this is hardly the end of the story. We hope you are inspired to use your newfound knowledge to improve the products and services under your management. After all, the previous 10 chapters have demonstrated that the immediacy of digitization is now imperative. We at Orbweaver have been privileged to see many companies profit and succeed as they align their people and systems for today's digital business needs. It is exciting to participate with companies on their journey of digital transformation, guiding stakeholders as they pursue goals and dreams that once seemed unreachable.

In partnering with so many industry-leading companies, we've observed that the range of problems and successes experienced by each vary greatly. In the face of transformative growth, challenges abound in the realms of personnel, budgeting, general execution, technology limitations, system inadequacies, security, and company culture, to name a few. With the potential breadth of people and processes impacted by the introduction of digital technologies and automated workflows, it is absolutely vital to clearly define your own success through measurable benchmarks and tangible goals.

Identifying and Revisiting Pain Points

First, consider the most common problems your organization experiences, and what alleviating them would mean. Delineate what needs solving, and what can remain in place. Remember: you have to crawl before you can walk—or run. When initiating a digital transformation, start small. Pick a minor and obvious burden at your organization that team members agree is burdensome. The unfortunate reality is that you will likely have several pain points from which to choose.

When evaluating a specific problem, be sure to meet with stakeholders who feel the pain most acutely. Perhaps it's a salesperson who hand-types quotes and purchase orders, or an IT staffer who toils endlessly to write part data file import macros. Find out exactly what they are spending too much time on, what they instead prefer to be focused on, and try to understand the tangible impact of this disconnect. As employees detail their challenges, attempt to sort those problems by pain vs. complexity.

Typically, you'll discover that at least a few of the challenges that are extremely painful and costly to your company are actually fairly simple to solve from a technical perspective. These are the optimal targets for kicking off your digital journey, because they will demonstrate high and immediate ROI, relative ease to remediate, and high probability of staff buy-in. From our experience, example areas include supplier data imports, purchase order intake and validation, and part data distribution to customers and/or distribution partners. Could one of these areas be a solid starting point for your digital initiative?

When we are embarking on a new journey, it often helps to learn from the experiences of other travelers. Here are some brief, specific examples of organizations that sought to remedy very specific pain points so they could ultimately improve operations, customer satisfaction, and overall profitability. How did some of our partners start? They took that first step toward resolution to meet industry demands.

Data Syndication: Advantech, a global leader in the manufacturing of high-quality, high-performance computing platforms, was feeling the negative effects of an inefficient, disorganized data distribution system. The organization was unable to find a "one-size-fits-all" solution to populate product information for disparate channel partners' systems. Through its partnership with Orbweaver, the company has simplified its procurement cycle and integrated data efficiently.

API Enablement: Cyient, which provides build-to-specification services for over 300 global customers, struggled to provide timely assemblies due to painfully slow inbound quote activity. After partnering with Orbweaver to improve response times for RFQs, the company is experiencing improved response, increased capacity--allowing more time to find source best price, and greater efficiencies overall. The organization is benefitting from improved operational speed as well as strategic agility.

Procurement Automation: Hammond Manufacturing is a global enterprise supporting electrical and electronic manufacturers' needs for power distribution, racks, and enclosures through a global network of agents and distributors. The company found that a lot of product information on distributors' websites was out of date, inconsistent, and ambiguous across channels. Fed up with endless "fixes," the company partnered with Orbweaver to improve its data distribution service through automation. The company is now selling more parts, thanks to its refined attribute data and its streamlined data distribution process.

These are just a few simple examples of how executing a digital initiative with a knowledgeable partner can yield substantial results in both process and profitability. Of course, every company has a unique set of pain points, company goals, and resources to manage these. But as leaders in data transformation and syndication in the electronics supply chain, we have contributed to numerous success stories. Next, we'll guide your start to digital transformation as you both solve everyday problems and create a vision for your participation in a future-proof digital supply chain.

Beginning Your Digital Transformation

Garnering Support

Once you've identified a starting point for your organization's digital initiatives, you will need two important things to proceed: the support of your peers and senior management, and an understanding of your in-house IT and system capabilities. Start conversations with these groups around the conference table, at the water cooler, or over a phone call. While digital evolution is necessary at this juncture in our industry, it's still vital to investigate employees' appetite for change. Initiate dialogue about the future of business, and how digital initiatives result in healthier, more profitable companies. More stability—and optimistically, success—for the company and all of its employees is a worthwhile goal.

Organizing and Planning

After identifying pain points, assessing IT systems, and garnering support, you may discover that the capabilities of your internal IT systems and/or bandwidth may not seem fully equipped or sufficient for tackling a large-scale initiative. Up until this point, your IT department has focused its energies on your company's core business systems and model, and rightfully so.

That's where third-party providers can step in to assist with specific, tactical efforts like enabling an API, translating EDI into your ERP, or importing quotes, purchase orders, forecasts, and part data, to name a few examples. These types of tasks, which cost a significant amount of time from an IT perspective without addition of much core value, are sensible candidates for third-party outsourcing. SaaS vendors can provide relatively inexpensive, low-overhead solutions that allow large organizations to avoid the insurmountable challenges of trying to turn their company into a software shop overnight. Even if a company has the in-house talent to create applications, they often do not have the infrastructure to support the SDLC. Beyond a certain point, internal development becomes an extremely costly and risky investment.

Regardless of your decision to implement an internal or external solution, take some basic measurements of the old system immediately before system deployment. Possible questions to consider include the following:

- How long do processes take to complete manually?

- What are the error rates?

- How happy are customers? How can you tell?

By taking measurements and gathering metrics, you'll have comparison points for the new initiative. Have a baseline understanding of what those key performance indicators (KPIs) were before rollout, so you can concretely evaluate the project's success.

Implementing and Deploying Solutions

With buy-in from your peers and management team, and the establishment of a champion (detailed in Chapters 1 and 6), you can begin the development and implementation process via a solution that fits your needs and specific pain point. Whether your solution is developed in house or with an external third party, remember to put a clear plan in place with goals and milestones. A clearly defined set of expectations among the implementation partner, management team, and your peers is vital. Set clear, short-term goals and even small experimental projects with an eye on the longer term.

Communicate early and often about where the initiative is headed and the most desirable outcome. Ongoing dialogue will enable an iterative process as the team demos various pieces of functionality and new processes through development. Visualizing mock-ups and discussing advantages, as well as potential areas for improvement, will help build excitement and establish an appropriate comfort level for all stakeholders throughout the implementation process. Once the solution is fully assembled, test it with the team of users. Find out if it meets their needs, confirming that it supports the resources already in place. Be prepared that while it may not be perfect on the first try, improvement over traditional, manual processing is the key goal.

Remind employees that those first steps of the digital initiative are not a destination or a switch that gets thrown. This is a journey toward meaningful, lasting change that will benefit the organization in a multitude of ways.

Re-Measuring and Evolving

After implementation of a new system, actively measure the metrics established before deployment to get a clear picture of recent improvements. Perhaps you'll see noteworthy gains in the speed with which you respond to clients; maybe you're able to respond more fully to a quote; maybe you're able to access your supplier data faster. Whatever that tangible data is, the primary effect of a digital initiative in this industry is the selling of more parts.

As processes are improved and sales increase, the initiative's positive results will encourage your organization to further expand its digital capabilities. Start looking for additional opportunities to apply digital solutions to nagging pain points or to evolve the solution you just deployed. As you evaluate measurable criteria by collecting ongoing metrics, don't be afraid to adjust the path of the overall digital transformation.

Ensuring Main Principles Are in Place

Digitization in the electronics industry begins with establishing —then adopting—a new business process that must be centered around a platform that supports the following primary principles.

Firstly, information must flow into the selected digital platform in an automated manner. The resources it requires to manually key in data is simply too costly. For example, receiving a PO and having an employee manually enter that into an ERP or MRP for fulfillment is a huge waste of time. The electronics industry, which is typically comprised of these small-sized transactions, cannot rely on that level of overhead moving forward. Automated intake of data is the only way to drive costs out of each transaction and to ensure profitability in any given circumstance.

Secondly, the resulting data and process must be transparent. With automation, all the required data is pulled into a centralized system for easy access and viewing. If all of a company's quoters happen to call in sick one day, a colleague or manager can view their work queue, see what quotes are new or in process, and easily continue the work to ensure a positive customer experience. The same transparency must hold for all data that flows into a company: RFQs, sales orders, change orders, shipping notices, invoices, and similar. These critical pieces of information are central to the selling or buying of parts and should be automated as they move in and out of a company.

Thirdly, the supporting data must be integrated. Having data stored in multiple systems is a real challenge for employees processing quotes, sales orders, or other key documents. These employees end up performing a lot of "copy and paste" just to process a request. Digitizing doesn't mean those systems have to be replaced; it means that the data should be integrated into a central platform so the process (or multiple processes) can be automated. For example, when a sales order is received, a salesperson must validate that the part number is correct, that the quantity on hand supports the requested buy, and that the delivery date is achievable. Typically, this requires logging in to multiple separate systems to gather information for validation. Integration of that required data would allow the sales order to be automatically validated against a series of rules and then processed.

If the data is valid, the sales order can flow directly into an ERP/MRP for fulfillment without a human having to touch it. If validation fails, "processing" might mean following up with the customer and adjusting the order for successful fulfillment. Digitization enables your talented, well-compensated teams to perform key strategic tasks for your company rather than spending valuable time manually entering and processing data.

Finally, data must be joined, or linked, together to generate analytics and valuable insights. As a result of the tenets above, the data necessary to automate and process intake of key documents is now accessible from a single, centralized system. Add to that the automated intake of the documents themselves, and a company can now clearly understand the success rate of quoting, the frequency of sales orders from a particular customer, or the number of exceptions or successes from a particular supplier or trading partner. Insights revealing demand by time of year or how it relates to large industry events or shifts can further support informed decision-making. With the centralization of information, the company can now make solid, educated decisions founded on current, actionable data.

Once your transformation is underway and these few tenets are met, consider your business processes *digital.* This process reveals company strengths and shortcomings--determinations that will vary from organization to organization. The outcome, however, is consistent across all organizations that engage in digital transformation: improved business processes, clear internal transparency, higher reliability of outcomes, satisfied customers, and a much more resilient and durable company. Do not dwell on any setbacks, but rather learn from the lessons digital transformation will provide. Most importantly, celebrate the wins and foster a proactive and positive environment around the productive change being generated.

Experiencing Transformation in Context

As organizations continue to establish plans for digital initiatives that future-proof their businesses, the pace of technological change in the industry, as a whole, is accelerating. The proliferation of APIs is spawning important conversations among suppliers and distribution partners globally. APIs—and other automated integration points—drive costs out of the sales and purchasing process, enabling profit margins to increase. They are now universally accepted as the path toward a more efficient, more resilient supply chain, and it's expected among trading partners that APIs will be incorporated.

Beyond APIs, blockchain and AI (as noted in Chapters 3 and 10) are also generating conversation in the context of how the next generations of technology will be applied in the industry. While their specific impact remains to be seen, digital transformation will include them. Organizations are expected to be ready and willing to adapt to emerging technologies, yielding the benefits of high-quality data applications through AI, blockchain, and analytics. Embracing these solutions for a digitized supply chain is absolutely essential to the health of our entire industry.

The democratization of data, designed to be extended, integrated, and incorporated into the industry's evolving technologies, will catapult the industry into the future. To keep pace with the ever-changing technical landscape, a third-party digital platform partner can guide your organization in identifying and applying technical solutions for maintaining efficient, customer-driven workflows in the buying and selling of parts. Remember, transformation is a capability, not a task that magically becomes "complete." The potential of the endeavor is truly extraordinary, and your journey has just begun.

Conclusion

It is an exciting and challenging time for the electronics industry. There are many opportunities to improve business processes and generate profits that were unthinkable in times past. There are also many challenges arising from increased competition, choppy market conditions, and an ever-changing landscape of technical progress. Standing still is not an option. We hope this book has provided some insights into the many considerations required for digital transformation. We wish you the best as you push the envelope and work to transform your company and its culture.

For More Information

To learn more about how Orbweaver can help, find the following resources online:

Orbweaver blog (https://www.orbweaver.com/blog/)

Orbweaver eBooks (https://www.orbweaver.com/resources/).

Made in the USA
Middletown, DE
16 February 2023

24177724R00139